THE PRESS WE DESERVE

THE PRESS WE DESERVE

edited by
Richard Boston

London   Routledge and Kegan Paul

First published 1970 by
Routledge & Kegan Paul Ltd,
Broadway House, 68–74 Carter Lane,
London E.C.4
Printed by The Camelot Press Ltd,
London and Southampton
© Routledge & Kegan Paul Ltd 1970

ISBN 0 7100 6821 2

Contents

Acknowledgments

The publishers wish to thank Mirage Music Ltd,, for permission to quote from 'Street Fighting Man' on page 125.

Introduction

This book was written in the second half of 1969, and throughout
the book examples, quotations and circulation figures are taken
from this period. (A few minor adjustments of up-dating were
made at proof stage, in February 1970.) Book production takes
time and newspapers change fast: inevitably there is a danger that
to some extent the book may have dated by the time it appears. I
hope not, and on the contrary suspect that some examples may
become sharper by being seen in the perspective of time.

I do not agree with every single word of every contribution to
this book; nor, I am sure, would all contributors agree with every
word of mine or of one another's. But we are in substantial agree-
ment, especially on the subject of advertising, and we are all critical,
more or less strongly, in one way or another, of the British press.

The plan of the book should be self-explanatory. Raymond
Williams sets the press of today in its historical context. D. A. N.
Jones, in his first contribution to the book, looks at the methods
and preoccupations of the press. Tom Baistow looks at its structures, and Malcolm Southan at the effects of advertising on
editorial content. Four chapters look at particular aspects of the
press – Susanne Puddefoot on women's journalism, Geoffrey
Nicholson on sport, John Palmer on financial journalism, and
D. A. N. Jones on reviewing. Peter Fryer looks at the dissenting, or
fringe, press, and A. C. H. Smith at provincial newspapers.
Finally Peter Brusse gives a foreign view of the British press.

Richard Boston

1

Growing pains

RICHARD BOSTON

Trees are fine, noble, beautiful things, and it was a shock to learn
that more than six million of them are felled every year to make
the newsprint for the *New York Times*, a single Sunday accounting
for the product of no less than 150 acres. Of course the Sunday
edition of the *New York Times* is notoriously vast, a seven-pounder
that comes in some fifteen sections, making our own *Sunday Times*
seem quite manageable by comparison. But as British papers
continue to proliferate sections and supplements it is clear that
they are evolving in the direction of the swollen monster of New
York. As my newsagent, who has had one heart attack already,
wakes me in the small hours by dropping through the front door
what sound like volumes of the *Encyclopaedia Britannica*, it
occurs to me that the objects lying in the hall bear the same
relationship to newspapers as a rubber glove, when tied to and
distended by the pressure of a mains water tap, bears to a human
hand.

The *News of the World* is physically smaller than the Sunday
edition of the *New York Times* but, as its circulation is much
bigger, it presumably accounts for a comparable quantity of
timber. And when you think of the deforestation that must be
going on in order to produce, *inter alia*, the *Daily Sketch* and the
News of the World and the *Sunday Mirror* and *The Times Business
News*, you might well wonder whether it's all worth it. But of
course you know it is. What are a few trees here and there against
a Free Press?

The words 'Free Press' are enough to clinch any argument. A Free Press is necessary for the preservation of Democracy. Everyone knows that. The Duke of Edinburgh, for example, says so in his Foreword to *Fleet Street: the inside story of journalism* (published by Macdonald & Co. for the Press Club in 1966): 'genuine democracy' he says (as opposed to the other sort of democracy, whatever that may be), 'can only flourish if it is exposed to the scrutiny of a free and uncensored Press'. The book in which the Duke puts forward this bold opinion is interesting only because it is a self-portrait of the established press. The cover of the book bears a photograph of the front pages of the *Daily Express, Daily Mail, Daily Mirror, Evening News, Daily Telegraph, Evening Standard, Sun, Daily Sketch, Guardian* and *The Times*. There it is, then, the Free Press, Democracy's Defender, represented by two London evening newspapers and all the national daily newspapers. All, that is, except the *Financial Times* which is a special case (it is, however, represented inside the book), and the *Morning Star*, or *Daily Worker* as it then was, which is a special case in a different way and appears neither inside nor outside the book. (As D. A. N. Jones commented when I pointed this out to him, the *Financial Times* and the *Morning Star* are the only papers which tell the truth about strikes.)

Sir Max Aitken, the Chairman of Beaverbrook Newspapers, says in his contribution to *Fleet Street*: 'There is nothing like a British newspaper. No institution in the world compares with it.' How true. Unfortunately these are not the words of a newspaper proprietor uniquely facing up to the gruesomeness of his product but on the contrary yet another example of Fleet Street's flatulent self-satisfaction. Sir Max continues: 'Reduced a little bit in numbers the Fleet Street newspapers today offer the public a complete range of opinion and expression totally free from outside direction . . .' 'Reduced a little bit in numbers' is a nice phrase; the rest of the sentence may serve as a useful statement of what the position is not.

A complete range of freedom and expression, in Sir Max Aitken's phrase, would presumably include, say, support for wildcat strikes, the legalization of marijuana, home rule for Scotland, war resisters who turn to direct action, Jack Dash, Miss Bernadette Devlin, students who try to take over their universities, hippies who take over empty houses and workers who take over their factories. These opinions, and a host of others that diverge from the bourgeois consensus, I do not remember having seen expressed in Fleet Street papers – except perhaps in a context that clearly labels the opinion as crackpot, and that, surely, is not allowing what Sir Max Aitken calls a complete range of *expression*.

The fact is that, to find anything like what Sir Max is talking about, the Fleet Street papers have to be supplemented first by the *Financial Times*, the *Morning Star*, *The Economist* and *Le Monde*, and then by, say, *Tribune*, *Private Eye*, *Peace News*, *IT*, *International Socialism*, *Freedom*, the *Black Dwarf* . . . obviously the range of opinion and expression (and information) would still not be complete, but it would already have been increased very considerably.

For Fleet Street, far from encouraging a diversity of opinion, on the contrary puts its full weight behind the pressure on individuals to conform. It viciously attacks dissent and divergence, whether these are political, moral or merely sartorial. As an example of the last, think of the way that for years Fleet Street has mocked, rebuked, cajoled and insulted the long-haired young. What the papers wanted, it might have been assumed, was short-haired young. Why, then, have the skinheads had such a bad press?

For Fleet Street's treatment of dissent from conventional middle-class *mores* think of the abuse that was hurled on Vanessa Redgrave, Yoko Ono and Marianne Faithfull for choosing not to marry the fathers of their expected babies. Even the usually fairly broadminded *Observer* took it upon itself to give Miss Redgrave a snotty-nosed editorial rebuke (which it later had the grace to retract). Recently the press's tone on this subject seems to have changed a little, if the coverage of the pregnancies of Mia Farrow and Caroline Maudling is anything to go by. But, even if less vituperative, the press's middle-aged interest in unwedlocked babies remains obsessively prurient.

Nor is the national press any more tolerant of political dissent. Consider the venomous attacks made on Bertrand Russell over the past few years: the *Daily Sketch* has perhaps been most consistently vicious here, but *The Times* has never been slow to put its grandiloquent boot in. For the full range of opinion does not apparently include such political positions as opposition to nuclear weapons, NATO, the Stock Exchange and so on. Nor does it include such criticisms of itself as I am making here, nor criticisms of its advertisers or indeed of the basic assumptions of the consumer society which it reflects and of which it is itself a part. The only drop-outs from the consumer society, the only individualists approved of by Fleet Street, are lone round-the-world sailors.

These, for reasons I do not pretend to understand, our newspapers, quality and popular – perhaps especially quality – feel to deserve unlimited, admiring attention.

*   *   *

Whenever a Fleet Street newspaper is threatened with closure there is a lot of talk about the danger to democracy that would be caused by the loss of a single newspaper. On the contrary I would argue that the *News of the World*, for example, or the *Daily Sketch* or *Sunday Mirror* is about as necessary to democracy as an outbreak of typhoid. Such papers may be the *price* of democracy, but that is rather a different matter.

Obviously I am not arguing that a free press is not necessary to a democracy. The press's importance was vividly demonstrated in Czechoslovakia in the year before and the year after the Russian invasion of August 1968, and also in Greece since the Colonels' *putsch* – to give but two examples. What I am saying is that the British press has come dangerously close to abrogating the responsibilities of a free press, that Fleet Street does not do precisely what Sir Max Aitken says it does, and for that reason it is not what the Duke of Edinburgh says it is.

As a fair indication of what *is* the range of the British press's interests, I have taken *The Times*'s headlines for six weeks immediately previous to the day on which I am writing (3 November 1969). I have taken *The Times* not because I think it is the best British newspaper (I don't) but because it will at least be generally agreed without too much argument that it is not the worst, and that I have therefore not made my job too easy for myself. I have also taken *The Times* as an example because, for good or ill, since the Thomson takeover, *Times* Newspapers (that is to say, *The Times* and *Sunday Times*) are where the action is. If they are not always typical of the press they do indicate more than any other papers the direction in which the rest of the press will in all probability follow.

Here then are *The Times*'s headlines for six weeks:

22 September	Squatters ousted by police commando
23 September	Peace plan in newspaper dispute
24 September	Go-ahead for US rival to Concorde
25 September	Bonn dispute over closing of markets
26 September	Vote against apartheid in S Africa
27 September	Bonn battle over mark goes on

29 September	Dr Kiesinger's small lead puts coalition plans in doubt
30 September	Brandt aims to form coalition with the Free Democrats
1 October	Wilson sets Labour party on road to general election
2 October	Jenkins sees a surplus of £450m
3 October	Six urged to act soon on Britain
4 October	Brandt set to become next Chancellor
6 October	Benn and Crosland move up
7 October	Heath comes down firmly for EEC
8 October	Heath issues orders for attack
9 October	Health men say rubbish is hazard
10 October	Minister in Benn team resigns
11 October	£2m deal to aid Ulster jobless
13 October	More troops go to Ulster after deaths
14 October	British Nato troops may go to Ulster
15 October	Boundaries bill to be abandoned
16 October	Millions take part in America's biggest anti-war protest
17 October	Press Council censure over Keeler series
18 October	Train robber flees as wife arrested in Melbourne
20 October	Polish plane hijacked by E Germans
21 October	Welsh plead for national coal strike
22 October	Pit pay deal accepted by union chiefs
23 October	US troops in Vietnam disengage
24 October	Conservative lead cut to 3·5 per cent
25 October	Mark revalued by 9·29 per cent
27 October	Labour faces new revolt on pay curb
28 October	Bonn softens its line on E Germany
29 October	Wilson to take new look at the prices law next year
30 October	Wilson attacked by Heath for drift to industrial anarchy
31 October	Swindon goes Tory on recounts
1 November	Hijack Boeing made to cross Atlantic

It is a typical set of headlines, and it is typically revealing. It shows, first, how little the British press is interested in what is going on in the rest of Europe, let alone the rest of the world. Out of the thirty-six headlines one-third do not immediately concern Britain. This proportion is not entirely discreditable until you look more closely at these 'foreign' headlines. Two out of the fourteen concern hijacked planes (another subject for which the press has an insatiable appetite). Seven of the foreign headlines concern Germany – and this, of course, was because the German elections were considered to be of unusual importance to Britain: a Social Democrat victory would (and did) mean revaluation of the Deutschmark, which would presumably put sterling in a less exposed position. Also it would mean German support for British entry into the Common Market (in fact the headline immediately following my sample, that for 3 November, read 'Brandt says early British–EEC talks are essential').

The German headlines are, then, something of a special case. Without them, and without the hijackings, we find that the rest of the world only managed to produce three out of thirty-six news items deemed worthy of front-page lead treatment: 'Vote against apartheid in S Africa', 'US troops in Vietnam disengage' and 'Millions take part in America's biggest anti-war protest'. (The train robber and Concorde headlines are merely foreign incidents in home stories.) This only confirms what is already well known – that the British press is often xenophobic and always insular. If you want a comprehensive coverage of foreign news you have to read *Le Monde*.

The large number of headlines about Germany is also typical of the 'fire-brigade' coverage favoured by the British press. It works something like this. There are widespread floods in Ruritania with appalling loss of life. The *Daily Brute* sends four of its top men – a reporter, who will later write a searing book on the subject; the economics editor, who will send reports on whether or not the disaster is serious enough to force the Ruritanian Schilling to devalue; the diplomatic editor, who will cover the Ruritanians' appeal to both Moscow and Washington for aid; and the business editor, who will report on the state of British investments in the country. After a few days the floods recede and rowing boats are no longer to be seen in the capital's thoroughfares. Mopping up will take months, perhaps years: the *Brute*'s reporter, indeed, writes that the real tragedy has not yet begun. But what is this that has caught the foreign editor's ever-watchful eye? Students are rioting in Urbania and it looks as though the fragile coalition government there is really in danger this time. The *Brute*'s crack team is ordered to leave Ruritania soonest and proceed Urbania urgentest.

This scenario is no exaggeration. One can see something like it in the coverage of Germany in my sample of headlines from *The Times*. Likewise Ulster gets three mentions, on three consecutive days. Then subjects disappear altogether. (Whatever *did* become of Anguilla?)

On 19 September, just before my sample began, *The Times* headline had read 'Marplan poll shows Social Democrats lead in Germany'. In the event the SPD got fewer votes than the Christian Democrats. Undeterred (and nothing will deter the press from polls), *The Times* announced on 24 October 'Conservative lead cut to 3·5 per cent'. But 31 October ('Swindon goes Tory on recounts') showed that the Tory lead in five by-elections the previous day was three or four times that. Poll stories are good examples of soft news (as opposed to the hard kind). By soft news I mean the speculation, comment and predictions that so often pass for news. Indicators of soft news in headlines are such words as *may, expected, faces, plans, aims,* of which instances will be found in the sample.

There are also the stories that are neither hard news nor soft, but are simply non-stories, or what Daniel Boorstin has called pseudo-events. 'Wilson sets Labour party on road to general election' sets a high standard of non-news early on in my sample, but it is easily beaten by three headlines that work up an inspired crescendo of banality: 'Six urged to act soon on Britain', 'Heath comes down firmly for EEC', and 'Heath issues orders for attack', any one of which could have appeared at any time in the last five (ten?) years. The last two are also examples of the well-known Heath-slams-Wilson syndrome: another is the delightful 'Wilson attacked by Heath for drift to industrial anarchy'.

The other side to the press's lack of interest in other countries is its parochialism. The headline 'Squatters ousted by police commando' is only one of the many that appeared day after day in the Fleet Street press last summer about the hippies who took over an empty building in Piccadilly. It was a story that was not entirely without interest, and one that would have deserved its front-page treatment in any local paper – but not surely in a national newspaper. This parochialism is further indicated by two headlines which are actually about newspapers themselves: 'Peace plan in newspaper dispute' and 'Press Council censure over Keeler series' (the latter story in all its stages perfectly fitted Boorstin's description of the making of a pseudo-event).

The British press is, then, not just nationally rather than

internationally minded. It is nationalistic, insular, parochial. We are often told that Britain is the only country in the world that has a national press. But we haven't got a national press. What we have is local newspapers that are nationally distributed. Fleet Street is a London press that gives London news and Londoners' views of the rest of the country. It is London events, London gossip, London exhibitions, plays and films that get discussed.

*   *   *

Recently, for purposes that had nothing to do with this book, I was looking through a copy of *The Observer* of some thirteen years ago. The issue of 24 February 1957 cost fourpence and had 16 pages. Ten years later (26 February 1967) it had doubled in price to eightpence and had gone up to 36 pages plus a 40-page colour supplement. The most recent issue at the time of my writing is 2 November 1969: the price has gone up another four-pence to a shilling, and there are 44 pages plus a 96-page colour supplement.

The Observer of 24 February 1957 would be distinguished if for no other reason than that it reported Miss Tallulah Bankhead as saying, 'I'm as pure as the driven slush'. But this was a happy accident, and the merits of the paper of that date rest on a more solid base. In some ways it was undeniably inferior to today's *Observer* – in terms of physical size for one. There were very few pictures at that time, and these were tiny and had extremely long captions. Two small photographs by Michael Peto on the front page were captioned: 'Two voters, both typically Welsh, pause in their work to listen to one of the candidates in the Carmarthen by-election. Note the intelligent faces, the attentive watchfulness. Every night since the campaign the three candidates have been drawing large audiences who look as deeply concerned as these two in the photographs.' It has about it a quaint period charm, has it not? Note, as the caption-writer might say, that the reader is told how to look at the pictures. Note that the reader is not expected to use his own eyes but to take the caption's word for it that the faces are intelligent. Note that, like the Bellman in 'The Hunting of the Snark', what the caption tells us three times is true: the faces are intelligent; they are attentively watchful; they look deeply concerned. Note finally that we are even told that we are looking at photographs, as though we might otherwise be fooled and think we had steel engravings in front of us.

The Observer of today is certainly far more visually sophisticated than that of thirteen years ago. But in other respects comparison favours the paper of 1957. It was a concise, tightly-packed paper in which important items – hard news, serious political comment, discussion of current artistic and cultural events – got about as much coverage as they do today, and the price was only a third. It is not hard to see where the expansion has taken place. The small feature on the City by 'Sterling' is the acorn from which has grown the mighty oak of today's 12-page pull-out *Business Observer*. Likewise the 1957 issue's column and a half on women's fashions by Alison Settle, the half-column on cooking by Syllabub, and half-column on travel have expanded into the colour supplements that are about as big as the telephone directory of a fair-size town – more readable perhaps, but less useful.

Today's *Observer* is a huge sprawling affair, a loose and baggy monster; perhaps somewhere inside it the paper of ten years ago is signalling wildly to be let out, but I fear that it is irrevocably lost in the welter of fashion, cookery, travel, potted history, gossip, briefing, background, insight, see-through, close-up, low-down, speculation and scuttlebut.

It seems to me that half a column on cooking is about the right amount for a good newspaper, and that even 1957's column and a half on women's fashions was probably too much. If you want more than that you can go and read *Elle* or some other specialist publication. But isn't it worth putting up with a lot of newsprint that can easily be discarded unread if it means that sometimes you get good material that you might otherwise not get? The answer to this is surely that even if subjects are treated perfectly seriously and intelligently in, say, a colour supplement (and they often are) they are trivialized by the context of endless advertisements for travel, motor-cars, fashion, domestic heating, carpets and sherry. Here at least one can agree with Marshall McLuhan. The colour supplement is a trivial medium, begat by advertising, and it can only trivialize its message. The obscenities of Vietnam and Biafra, beautifully photographed in colour, become simply what we read before getting to the cookery recipes and the holiday guide.

It may seem unfair to pick on *The Observer* when the *Sunday Times* is even huger and even more sprawling. But a comment on today's *Observer* is bound to be harsh simply because in the mid-1950s it used to be such a very excellent paper. Many people who are now between about twenty-five and thirty-five will remember Sundays in the years before and after Suez when they read *The*

B

Observer from cover to cover. It seemed to be a paper conceived in such a way that everyone could read all of it (I never failed to read Syllabub; I well remember his recipe for grass). For us at that time, absurd though it may now sound, *The Observer* was a beacon in intellectual, political and cultural affairs, our guide, philosopher and friend. Perhaps there are eighteen-year-olds today who read *The Observer* in the way we did then, but it somehow seems improbable.

Because it used to be so good, its physical growth has distorted *The Observer* more painfully than any other paper (the *Sunday Times* in those days was a stodgy dish of Field Marshals' memoirs). When *The Observer* opposed the Suez invasion it behaved with the courage and responsibility that, if it were more common, would enable one to take more seriously the press's self-important descriptions of itself as the Fourth Estate. But *The Observer* has had to pay for its courage, in hard commercial terms, ever since. I have no doubt that if another Suez were to occur (it is hard to imagine what form another Suez would take) *The Observer* would again take a courageous responsible line. But it would no longer be able to survive such a crisis. If today it suddenly lost thousands of readers, as it did at the time of Suez, it would also lose advertisers, and all those supplements would immediately become very expensive liabilities.

The editorial content of enormous newspapers like the Sunday edition of the *New York Times*, or our less enormous but still unnecessarily big Sunday newspapers, is obviously shaped by advertising. No sane, let alone responsible, editor could *want* to give more space to dollies' clothes fashions than to Vietnam. He does so because a feature about dollies' clothes will attract large advertisements from dollies' clothes manufacturers, while stories about Vietnam only attract a few column inches from Oxfam and War on Want. One contributor to this book after another turns sooner or later to the subject of advertising, and all are concerned at the dominant position of advertising in the press.

Most newspaper readers probably do not realize the extent to which what they read is controlled by advertising. This happens in all sorts of ways. For example, if there is one page of book reviews in your paper today whereas there were two pages last week, it would be naïve of you to suppose that more books of interest were published in the first week: there were simply more advertisements, and so there was also more space for editorial matter. Fewer ads means fewer reviews.

A literary journalist who was once a colleague of mine used to shake his wise head over this and say that it was not a situation that occurred anywhere else in the paper: 'They tell the literary editor he can't have any more space because there aren't enough book ads, but they don't tell the news editor that he can't have space to report a hanging unless they get an ad from a hemp rope manufacturer,' he would say. In fact he was not altogether right, for the principle that applies on news pages is the same as that on books pages. If there were three news pages in your newspaper yesterday, and today there are only one and a half it is not because less has happened in the world but because there are fewer ads.

Because newspapers, especially quality newspapers, have become more and more dependent on advertising, the editor has been forced to surrender much of his independence to the advertising manager. The editor has to give coverage to what brings ads, and it sometimes seems that he can't afford much space for things that merely bring readers (as Geoffrey Nicholson points out, sport is something that brings a paper readers but not ads). Today's newspapers look more and more as if they have been dreamt up by the advertising and management departments of a newspaper. Lord Thomson's phrase about editorial matter being the stuff between the ads seemed shocking when he first used it, but it is now beginning to look like a truism.

The size and power of the advertising and management departments of newspapers in recent years has increased, is increasing and ought to be diminished. Newspapers are no longer run by journalists but by jumped-up accountants, lawyers, printers and such like. It is in the highest levels of newspaper management that there is the grossest incompetence, and it is there that the power, the prestige and the money lie. (On the question of money alone, Cecil King's 'emoluments' in his last year as chairman of the International Publishing Corporation were £35,000.)

There are two possible approaches to a solution of this problem. One is a solution from above: that is to say by Act of Parliament. D. A. N. Jones in his chapter 'What's news?' makes a proposal along just such lines.

The other approach to the problem, which I am personally more interested in (though it does not in any way conflict with a parliamentary solution) is to work from below. Newspapers should be run by journalists. The present managements and proprietors, however, are not going to hand the papers over just for the asking. Journalists will have to become far more militant. At the moment, compared with the printers for example, their position is absurdly exposed. Management can fire an editor, against the wishes of his staff, without difficulty. They would never be able to fire a SOGAT member so easily. It seems obvious that journalists should be just as well protected as other members of the industry.

The formation of the Free Communications Group has helped to give some focus to this area of discussion. Its publication *Open Secret* has, as well as blowing the gaff on London Weekend Television, reported the steps taken on papers in France and Germany towards some form of journalistic control of newspapers. On *Stern*, West Germany's biggest illustrated magazine, the journalists threatened to strike rather than work for a new proprietor, and they thereby prevented an unpopular takeover. They also won the right to elect an editorial committee of seven members: without a two-thirds endorsement from this committee the chief editor cannot be hired or fired and none of the editorial staff can be dismissed.

In France the journalists of *Le Figaro* went on strike for nearly three weeks last year over the principle that editorial and administrative control of a newspaper should be independent of ownership. On *Le Monde* the journalists (in the form of the Société des Rédacteurs) own forty per cent of the equity and have veto powers over important matters. More than thirty papers in France have followed *Le Monde*'s example.

Eventually there will have to be action here by journalists to take control of their papers. Until the British press ceases to be dominated by management and advertising it will continue to be what the underground calls the Unfree Press. And at present it is the fringe press, the underground, counter-culture press (perhaps dissenting press is the best word) that carries out many of the responsible duties that are left undone by the established press. (Fleet Street, incidentally, has done singularly little to defend the dissenting press from the persistent harassment it has received.) The three great success stories of journalism since the war are *I. F. Stone's Weekly*, *Le Canard Enchaîné* and *Private Eye*. This statement is not intended to be merely provocative. Each of these publications regularly provides information that can be found nowhere else. Two of them, *I. F. Stone's Weekly* and the *Canard*, contain no advertising at all.

*   *   *

Aylmer Maude tells us that Tolstoy 'never read newspapers and considered them both useless and injurious, since they constantly propagate false news and erroneous ideas . . . He believed that the Press had been degraded, and its true mission lost sight of, by the publication for gain of much that is unnecessary.' The comment is even truer now than it was in Tolstoy's time. *Le Monde* is an exception and might be taken as a model of what a paper should be. The nearest to an exception in this country is the *Guardian*. Otherwise, apart from the dissenting press, it is hard to think of papers that do not merely, in Wordsworth's phrase, gratify the craving for extraordinary incident, and are not guilty (in Tolstoy's phrase) of publication for gain of much that is unnecessary.

We have a choice. Either the press should be run on business lines, subject to market and commercial forces, and have as its prime aim the making of money by selling more copies and getting more advertisements. That is more or less what Fleet Street is today, and conservatives can, if they want to, logically defend it as such. In that case, however, they should drop the claptrap about the Fourth Estate and the defence of democracy. Businessmen should not give themselves such airs.

Alternatively the press should be conceived of as a social service – the rapid communication by printed means of information and opinions. As such, profit should be a secondary motive. Indeed, there is no reason why a newspaper that is run as a social service should 'pay' at all. We do not expect profit to be the main object of other social services – of roads or schools or hospitals, for example. If such a proposal is charged with Utopianism, the answer is the same as to all such accusations. If we try to reach Utopia and fail, we will at least have been travelling in the right direction.

2

Radical and/or respectable

RAYMOND WILLIAMS

Many people, when they talk about the popular press, seem to miss the most important question of all: are these papers written *by* ordinary people, or merely *for* them? Ordinary perhaps begs a question. In all societies we know about, public writing of any kind, including journalism, is a minority activity; the people who do it are in that sense out of the ordinary. But there is another way of looking at it, which is very important in the history of the popular press. The people writing and distributing particular newspapers can be, in their basic circumstances and condition of life, very close to their readers; or, obviously, they can be living very differently but writing for what they imagine or discover to be the interests of others. In fact, unless we make this distinction, we cannot discuss the popular press in any truly critical way; we cannot look at the structures which determine the kind of writing and communication it is.

In our own time there are two kinds of newspaper which are based on a comparatively simple and visible social structure. The first is what is called, in distinction from popular, quality: meaning not, I suppose (or not just like that) that it is read by 'the quality', but that it takes for granted a known set of subjects and interests, based for the most part on a roughly common level of education. There are often errors and failures inside this assumption, but it is still fairly easy to see when editors and writers are taking it for granted that their readers are people living much like themselves. Significantly one of the current difficulties in these newspapers is that for commercial reasons they are trying to expand, continually, this assumed community, and are often tempted past its realities to that kind of promotion which is the conscious suggestion of fashions and trends. 'The sort of people who . . .' extends from a reasonable description to an advertising manager's hope or trick.

Still, when we say 'their readers' we mean something different from current popular papers' attitudes to 'their' readers. What would happen, for example, if *The Times* or the *Guardian* head-lined their correspondence columns 'You Write' or 'You're Telling Us'? It is a simple enough check: we know whether we have written and told them or not. But 'you' within a real community of interest is still specific, and the impersonality of 'Readers' Letters' is then a form of politeness. 'You' in the modern popular paper, on the other hand, means everyone who is not us: we who are writing the paper for 'you' out there. There are often blurred edges, but the line between those papers which assume a kind of community – in this society, inevitably, either a social class or an educational group – and those which assume quite different relationships – readers seen as consumers, as a market or potential market – is not too difficult to draw, and is usually directly visible in layout and style.

The second kind of modern newspaper in which there is a com-paratively simple and visible social structure is the local paper: under some pressures, certainly, and with several contradictory features of chain ownership and monopoly; but still normally expressing a common experience which is there quite apart from the newspaper itself: of living in a particular place, sharing certain local needs and interests, facing certain local problems. The style of local newspapers – in journalistic terms often 'old-fashioned' – expresses at least this minimum level of known identity and relationship. It quite often abuses this sense of community, for political reasons, but as a structure it is still of the general kind I am offering to distinguish. The paper is to an important extent written *with* people if not *by* them; and in the sense that it is written *for* them this can be defined, quite reasonably, in terms of an interest larger than the paper itself: the interest of the local community.

It is with this perspective in mind that we can look at the history, in Britain, of the 'popular' press. I don't mean to repeat the story of its general development, which is already recorded. But I want to analyse, in a preliminary way, what seems to me its most critical feature: the transition from an independent popular press to a commercial popular press, looking particularly at what happened in the nineteenth century, as a way of seeing, with some edge, what is happening in our own time. I need to begin by insisting – I had thought it was no longer necessary but a recent popular history disabused me – that the key to this development is *not* the Education Act of 1870. There were more than enough readers, before that Act, to sustain the present circulation of the *Daily Mirror*; and there were also, before the Act, both kinds of popular newspaper, the independent and the commercial. It is the 'consumer' or 'market' kind of thinking, now endemic in journalism, which led to this false interpretation. For the problem is not the number of readers, or potential readers, in simple quantitative terms. The question about any medium of communication is a question about its social structure: its actual and possible organization and relationships. Of course the growth of literacy underlay the extension of the press, but that growth itself is a steadily rising curve through the whole of the nineteenth century, with no particular peak at 1870 or at the date of the Act's effects in the 1880s. The real social history is more interesting, and is of course profoundly connected with very general political and economic developments.

No simple summary can be adequate, but the way of seeing this history that I want now to suggest is, first, the emergence of an independent popular press, directly related to radical politics, in the first decades of the nineteenth century; second, the direct attack on this, and its attempted suppression, in the period up to the 1830s though with some later examples; and third (and most important, as a way of understanding our own situation) the indirect attack, by absorption but also by new kinds of commercial promotion, which aimed not at suppressing the independent popular press but at *replacing* it, in fact by the simulacrum of popular journalism that we still have in such vast quantities today. I shall need also to consider, briefly, the situation of the surviving independent press in the period, down to our own day, in which this commercial replacement had occurred and become successful and even rampant.

*   *   *

The emergence of independent radical newspapers in the first decades of the nineteenth century has been well documented by, among others, Aspinall (*Politics and the Press, 1780–1850*),

Wickwar (*The Struggle for the Freedom of the Press 1819–1832*), Webb (*The British Working Class Reader*) and Altick (*The English Common Reader*), and is well set in its political context by Thompson (*The Making of the English Working Class*). As we read the working lives of Cobbett and Wooler and Carlile and Hetherington and so many others like them, we can begin to realize what political prejudice is when men like Northcliffe get celebrated as pioneers. These are the real heroes of popular journalism, and to understand it we must turn first, not to *Tit-Bits* and *Answers* and the halfpenny *Daily Mail*, but to the *Political Register*, the *Black Dwarf*, the *Voice of the People*, the *Poor Man's Guardian*, the *Poor Man's Advocate*, the *Working Man's Friend*, the *Destructive*. The relationship indicated in the majority of these titles is probably the most important thing about them; it was Cobbett who said in 1820:

> I have derived from the people . . . ten times the light that
> I have communicated to them . . . It is the flint and the
> steel meeting that brings forth the fire.

Certainly, of course, it is a political relationship. That is what allows these papers to be dismissed, in a later and very different consciousness, as specialist or sectarian. But we have to consider the situation, now indeed very difficult to imagine, in which there was no organized commercial establishment or even political system claiming to embody or to represent the people's interests. The independent popular press was staking a new claim, articulating a new voice, in a situation in which otherwise there would have been silence. This gave the radical journalists a certain obvious initiative, though that is a very passive way of describing what had to be fought for, at real and substantial personal risk, every column-inch of the way. Yet the sense of initiative is still critically important. Anti-popular or pseudo-popular journalism had to enter a field already occupied, as the reactionary *White Dwarf* for example makes clear. The established newspapers were simply not written for, not even considering, the people who became Cobbett's and Wooler's and Hetherington's readers.

Who were these readers, and where had their writers come from? By the 1820s and 1830s there is a clear social identity, in the radical popular press. The writers had varied histories, and because they were imprisoned and persecuted they were forced into the profession of radical editor as much as they chose it. But as we look at their lives, we find that they were textile workers, booksellers, printers, small farmers, artisans. And what we know about their readers, from the evidence of many local centres, indicates a very similar social group: the artisans, small independent tradesmen and skilled workers.

The circulation varied, of course, with the rise and fall of the political temperature. Cobbett, at his peak, sold from forty to sixty thousand copies; the *Black Dwarf* reached 12,000; other radical weeklies, especially in the 1830s, between fifteen and thirty thousand. These are small figures, at first sight, to be described as 'popular'. But as with all papers of the period, and perhaps especially with these, the number of actual readers was very much greater than the number of copies sold. Clubs, coffee-houses, barber-shops and political groups bought for collective readership. The distribution of the papers was in itself an act of social and political organization. Moreover, comparatively, this popular radical press was in its successful period well ahead of the middle-class newspapers. *The Times* had a contemporary circulation of about 5,000, though it rose at times of political crisis to about 15,000.

The competition between these two kinds of paper was of course not abstract. It occurred in a political context. At the beginning of the nineteenth century the political establishment was still hostile to newspapers of any kind. As the Tory *Anti-Jacobin Review* put it in 1801:

> We have long considered the establishment of newspapers in this country as a misfortune to be regretted; but, since their influence has become predominant by the universality of their circulation, we regard it as a calamity most deeply to be deplored.

This was before the establishment of the radical popular press, which then met not only alarm but conscious authoritarian action to suppress it. In an earlier phase, the development of any newspapers had been hindered by special political taxes – the advertisement and stamp duties; and these were raised, repeatedly, as the influence of the press became more important. Direct bribes – 'subsidies' – were given to newspapers willing to take the government's side; similar bribes were given to journalists; government advertising was used in a discriminatory way, being placed only in politically subservient or safe papers. But these market measures were mainly ways of dealing with the middle-class press. Against the popular press measures were more direct, though some of the same instruments were used. Lord Ellenborough commented on the measures directed against the press in the Six Acts of 1819:

> It was not against the respectable Press that this Bill was directed, but against a pauper press . . .

The comment has a cold viciousness. Pauperization was indeed what was intended. When the popular press fought back, as in the campaigns of the 'Great Unstamped', the power of the law was used repeatedly and directly. Carlile and Hone, Cobbett and Hetherington and others were prosecuted and imprisoned. And action was taken not only against writers and editors, but locally and often more brutally against sellers and distributors. Of all periods in British history, that between 1815 and the 1830s is outstanding for its struggle for freedom of the press: not just the respectable struggle for commercial independence, though in the end that was important; but the struggle in the streets, the little shops, the clubs: men keeping their own publications going, one way or another, against an openly repressive and arbitrary regime.

Who can then wonder, if this was the situation, that this popular press was political? It is not a matter of sectarian choice. It is a struggle to speak and to live, against a State power which was prepared to use any method to oppose and to repress democratic activity. But then this open authoritarianism combined with the absence of any safe popular press to give these radical papers their identity and their authority. In later periods this defining situation was to change, and a new phase of the popular press then began.

*   *   *

The radical popular press, though harassed and poor, did not disappear from the culture. In the Chartist period, it went through an important new period of activity and vitality, and from that day to this there have always been papers expressing unorthodox or unestablished political opposition. In our own century, the *Herald* and the *Worker*, *Tribune* and the *Morning Star*, the new *Black Dwarf* and many others, are the direct descendants of that heroic period. But some elements of their situation have decisively changed. State action against them has not exactly been absent; the law is still used in some extreme cases. But the critically different element is the existence of a commercial popular or pseudo-popular press, against which the political papers of the opposition or the underground are measured and have to measure themselves.

The stages of this development are extremely complicated. The most important factor, perhaps, is the popular Sunday paper. Most histories of British journalism concentrate on the daily press, tracing a line from *The Times* through the 1855 *Telegraph* through the 1896 *Mail* to the twentieth-century *Express* and *Mirror*. That is a real history, marked by stages of political reform (the basis for the first success of *The Times*), of abolition of the market taxes (the direct origin of the *Telegraph*), of new kinds of advertising revenue (the *Mail*), and throughout by important technical developments, from the steam press to linotype, and by changes in distribution facilities, notably with the coming of the railways.

But there is another history, at first more relevant to the fate of the popular press. In a time of high prices the Sunday paper was always more widely read than the dailies; moreover it appeared on the working man's one day of leisure. From the early nineteenth century the Sunday papers led in circulation and popularity, as indeed they do to this day. And what went into these Sunday papers was popular in a quite different sense from that of the radical press. The *Political Register*, the *Black Dwarf*, the *Poor Man's Guardian* were almost exclusively political: that was their popular basis, a new radical consciousness. But the Sunday papers drew on a different popular consciousness. Though usually radical in such political news and commentary as they included, papers like the *Dispatch* and *Bell's Life in London*, and from the early 1840s *Lloyd's Weekly* and the *News of the World*, added two elements which were eventually to predominate: reports of crime and of sport, 'Combining, with the News of the Week, a rich Repository of Fashion, Wit and Humour, and the interesting Incidents of Real Life', as *Bell's Life in London* described itself in the 1820s. But even so, at that period the political news was important, and the circulation, at about 10,000, was in the same world as that of the radical weeklies. In the 1840s, this situation decisively changed. 'Extraordinary Charge of Drugging and Violation' was the leading headline of the first *News of the World*. 'Daring Conspiracy and Attempted Violation' announced *Bell's Penny Dispatch*, and its subtitle was 'Sporting and Police Gazette, and Newspaper of Romance'. Circulations rose rapidly, to fifty and then to a hundred thousand, and within forty years to a million. This is the phenomenon which alters the whole definition of 'popular'.

In certain important ways, this was not new material. Whereas the daily paper and the political weekly, respectable and/or radical, derived in tone, layout and style from the printed book and from the magazine tradition which had grown out of it, the new Sunday papers derived from what had long been the main popular reading matter: the chapbook, the printed ballad, the pamphlet and the last dying speech. Some of the radical journalists had used some of these elements, notably in political caricature. But the systematic remaking and regularization of these methods was carried out in the Sunday papers, and put on a new basis.

It is easy to see this, looking back, as exploitation. This is undoubtedly what it eventually became. The popular radical press, as Cobbett above all reminds us, was written in everyday language, with colour, vitality and force; very often without the restraints and qualifications of highly educated writing. And this is sometimes a style difficult to distinguish from what became the staple of commercial popular journalism, which used every device of language and layout to attract attention quickly and to excite known interests. But in the main the difference is clear: the radical style is one of genuine arousal; the commercial style is one of apparent arousal as a cover for an eventual if temporary satisfaction. Many variants can be seen between these two extreme kinds. One interesting example is Reynolds, a Chartist who published a relatively unsuccessful Chartist periodical, and a radical journalist, using the new Sunday paper (*Reynolds' News* as it survived until almost our own time) as a combination of radical opinion and what can best be called radical scandal: the vices of courts and high society in general. What is crucial, at that time, is that radical social and political attitudes (whether real, as in Reynolds, or functional, as in some others) were still an essential ingredient of this kind of popular paper. Between the 1840s and 1850s, when this is still clearly so, and our own period, when some of the most characteristic papers of this kind are also, politically, the most crudely reactionary, the critical transformation was made. Signs of the stance persist, as in the title of *The People*, but in general what had once been popular, in the political sense, was absorbed or deflected into 'popular' in quite other senses.

What happened, basically, was that in this decisive area market journalism replaced the journalism of a community or a movement. It is easy to conclude that the explanation lies in popular taste: the scandalous papers were what the public preferred. But the situation in which this happened was to a large extent determined. Two conscious attempts had been made to defeat the independent popular press: the period of open repression, up to the 1830s; and the period of specific replacement, most evident in the educational and family magazines between the 1830s and the 1850s – safe and instructive popular writing, from a middle-class point of view. Each had its important effects. The repression, though bravely fought, was at times crippling and even exhausting. The replacement, which includes some genuine and valuable work among a mass of quite open manipulation, made its way especially among the serious and conscientious readers who had been the basis of the radical press and its main hope for decisive expansion. But in our justified attention to these two phases, we can overlook the more effective movement, which was never so consciously (if at all consciously) intended, but which in reflecting certain real economic and social developments acquired an almost irresistible power.

Popular culture is always an uneasy mixture of two very different elements: the maintenance of an independent popular identity, often linked with political radicalism, resistance to the establishment, and movements for social change; and ways of adapting, from disadvantage, to a dominant social order, finding relief and satisfaction or diversion inside it. So complex is this, as a human process, that the elements often overlap and combine. But what the Sunday papers spoke to, with increasing effect, was the second element, which they both supplied and reinforced. A political radicalism, often deliberately isolated and made defensive, was then in constant danger of separating out from the popular culture as a whole: of being seen as, and of being, sectarian and strange.

This difficulty would have occurred in any event. It is part of the history of all popular movements, when the political element separates out and comes to seem, on its own, narrow or even alien. But economic circumstances vastly increased this difficulty. In the early decades, a man with a hand-press and friends could run a newspaper. The political definition created its own self-sustaining distribution system. None of the established papers was then very different in kind, since all distribution was slow and capital requirements, before new machines, were still not large. But when, as from the 1840s, really rapid commercial distribution on a national scale became possible through the railways, the situation was decisively altered. A market was competing with a self-sustaining movement. And when new printing techniques really began to be used on a wide scale, the independent editor and writer were quickly put at a major disadvantage. From this time on, access to capital, steadily growing in amount, was a condition of really successful popular journalism. *The Times* owed much of its early lead to steam-printing, and as competition increased for a rapidly expanding market the scale of necessary capital rose continually. Until the 1880s most newspapers still remained independent single enterprises, though on a middle-class rather than, as earlier, on a craftsman scale. From the 1880s on, two new elements – the organization of groups of newspapers and magazines, enabling more efficient and continuous use of the new machines; and the successful bid for really large-scale advertising revenue, in the commodity stage which the economy had then reached – pushed the whole organization of the press into a wholly new phase. From this time on, independent popular papers could only struggle at the margin. The control of popular journalism passed into the hands of successful large-scale entrepreneurs, who alone now could reach a majority of the public quickly and attractively and cheaply, on a national scale, but who by their very ability to do this, by their control of resources, were separated from or opposed to the people whom this popular journalism served. These fundamental economic developments achieved more, in the displacement of the independent popular press, than either the repression or the conscious substitution.

*   *   *

The pressures of the new economic situation then deepened the contradiction within popular culture which we have already referred to. It has always been possible to maintain a radical opposition or underground press, through the voluntary work and the sacrifices of people dedicated to its political aims. In the nineteenth century, as in our own, these papers kept coming, in direct relation to great popular movements, from the Chartist *Northern Star* and *The People's Paper*, through local papers like the *Midland Counties Illuminator*, to the *Clarion* and *Commonweal* of the socialist 1880s and 1890s. In the twentieth century, a strike sheet in a printing dispute in 1911 grew into the *Daily Herald* and in the 1920s attempted to challenge the capitalist press on its own terms: running with real success but eventually drawn down into a competitive market. The last years of the *Herald* (to say nothing of the *Sun*), or of *Reynolds' News* and the renamed *Sunday Citizen*, show the contradiction very sharply. The political newspaper has to compete within a structured market, and against certain defined popular expectations of newspapers. The development of the *Daily Worker* into the *Morning Star* is a still active example of this continuing difficulty.

What the opposition or underground press can always reach and serve is its own already structured or potentially structured public. Anyone who moves in active radical circles has available to him a press of bewildering variety, often sharply and internally polemical, which is at once an active and indispensable part of minority political organization. But he has only to move outside these circles (if only on holiday) for this whole active press to disappear as if it had never existed. And for the majority of people this is the normal situation, in spite of repeated and dedicated efforts to overcome it by street-selling and canvassing. The radical minority press is thus effectively isolated, though it is ironic that it is assiduously read (the only readers outside its own organizations) by the authorities and by professionals in commercial popular communications, who indeed make use of it, in their different ways.

The pressure of this situation leads to considerable internal disputes. For radical writers are aware, as Cobbett and Carlile and the others did not have to be, of a pseudo-popular press going into every home. It is an ironic reversal of Eldon's authoritarian alarm, in 1819:

> There was scarcely a village in the Kingdom that had not its little shop in which nothing was sold but blasphemy and sedition.

For 'blasphemy and sedition' read – what? 'confusion and prejudice'; 'manipulation and distraction'; 'pap'?

Three reactions are then possible: the maintenance of opposition and underground papers, come what may, in the hope of extension; the combination of opposition and underground policies with elements of the commercial popular culture – certain kinds of featured sport or featured sex; or the parallel or sometimes separate permeation of the respectable press, which of course includes some radical elements and which at times, in any case, needs to include radical and underground news and voices. None of these courses or decisions is easy, and the dispute about them is not going to be quickly resolved. When Cobbett attacked 'the bloody old *Times*' for its support of repression of the field-labourers' risings in the early 1830s, he was fighting on relatively equal terms and could point to *The Times* as self-evidently the voice of a different social class. To attack today the bloody old *Mirror* or the bloody old *Express* or the bloody old *News of the World* is not only to fight on unequal terms but in a situation in which the voice of a different social class, factually quite clear in ownership and political opinion, has, by hiring and practice, been made to sound popular; indeed often more popular, by assiduous imitation, than the strained and excluded voices of the Left.

This has determined my own emphasis: on the structure of majority communications, and on ways of changing that, radically, by pressure from without and within. But of course I do not suppose that this is an easier or more obviously successful course than any of the others I mentioned. What is at issue, really, is a much wider question of popular culture. It is easy to see, looking either back or around, that many elements of popular culture have been distractions from social reality, or subservient adaptations to it. The new urban culture contemporary with the nineteenth-century papers shows this distraction and adaptation as clearly as it shows independent response and revolt. The new music-halls of the 1840s and onwards are an excellent example: they included not only the new working-class and popular performers, responding to and entertaining within an everyday urban life, but also the plush and tinsel and the Champagne Charlies of the metropolitan escape and fashion-gaping. The pop world of the 1960s is structurally very similar, containing authentic and independent new sounds and experiences directly alongside the plush and tinsel and the fashions (some of it, surely, must be the same tinsel, as some of it is certainly the same saccharine). Commercial sport, active since the 1850s, contains the same divergent elements, of direct and independent performance and enjoyment, with a real communal life supporting it, and a displacement into money and star values, an adaptation of protest (including, significantly, many actual protest songs) into marginal and easily discharged conclusions and satisfactions. This is how, at many levels including the popular press itself, a popular culture has been mediated, within certain dominant and persistent social and economic forms, and within the kind of resignation to them which does not exclude widespread scepticism and frequent local hostility.

That mediation, I am sure, will have to be broken from within,

c

by people who not only value but share what is living and active inside it, and who can at the same time distinguish what is false and empty and manipulative. But of course it is ironic that one then writes this in a book, when what is needed, obviously, is a popular press: even one paper to start with. It will be an extraordinary struggle to get to that point, and a quite different struggle from that of the first radical editors and the Great Unstamped. Still, we ought not only to think of them as pioneers and as heroes; the simpler figures of a heroic time. When we look at what they did and what they risked, we should be decent if we did only half as much.

3

What's news?

D. A. N. JONES

Who is it for?

What's the news of the world? 'That was *the world* at 1.30,' claims the BBC. 'All human life is there,' boasts the *News of the World*. 'It puts the whole world in your grasp,' runs an advertisement for the *Sunday Telegraph*. Obviously, each of these media is selecting from an immeasurable quantity of recent events in the world, choosing news stories which they expect to appeal to the consumers and/or advertisers. The news is what newspapers choose to tell us about, in the same way that intelligence is what intelligence tests tell us about.

We do not all read the same news. We are divided by advertisers into two classes, according to our purchasing power and related characteristics, such as education and leisure habits. The newspapers designed for the wealthier minority, whether their opinions be conservative or liberal, offer different news items from those selected by the mass-circulation press. There are several euphemisms for the minority newspapers (*Guardian*, *Times*, *Telegraph*, etc.) – 'serious', 'literate', 'quality'; what they have to do is to sell a certain quantity of expensive goods, whereas the popular papers have to sell a much larger quantity of cheaper goods.

Compare two quality newspapers, the *Guardian* and the *Sunday Telegraph*, with two popular newspapers, the *Daily Mirror* and the *News of the World*. Each of the qualities holds 'opinions' close to one of the populars – but in the selection of news items, the qualities have much more in common with each other. It is a mark of being 'serious' to devote a great deal of space to party politics – on the reasonable ground that the wealthier, longer-educated section of the community is the more accustomed to generalizing on such matters, and more likely to be personally involved. One of the marks of a popular newspaper wishing to be considered as a quality (to attract a different class of advertising) is that it gives more space – and *emphasis* – to political stories. The London *Evening Standard* is the most successful of those papers attempting to bridge the gulf between quality and popular: the reason is that it has only one rival, the London *Evening News*, chosen by most working-class Londoners. Thus the *Standard* is enabled to win the quality advertisements. That is why its front-page lead on 16 September 1969 was 'NIXON'S CALL: "END THIS WAR"'; whereas the *News* led with 'MOUNTAIN BOY, FATHER LOST ON DEATH PEAK'.

Theology used to be known as the queen of the sciences, long after most scholars had lost interest in this discipline. Similarly, 'politics' – in the sense of politicians' doings and sayings – is queen of the news. Lip-service is paid to politics, in spite of the knowledge that, to put it mildly, few readers turn first to the political news. Many will find their news among the advertisements. *The Times* may have a report on a political action by the South African government, with perhaps a critical comment; but some of the readers will think more important the news offered in an advertisement (a company statement) in the paper's *Business News* section: 'In South Africa, profits are being consistently made, the order book is very healthy, and we are considering further expansion.' Advertisements are often a kind of news, most obviously advertisements for jobs and accommodation. It is a convenience to employers and estate agents (and, to be fair, their clients) to have the press divided between two classes of readership: the press is a product of the 'two nations' situation and helps to perpetuate it.

Among the news items peculiar to the quality press are reports of the sports which readers played at school and university, old boys' reunions, academic successes, luxuries (foreign hotels and West End theatres), births and deaths among the wealthiest – and, of course, investments. The hard-line popular press cannot cover this. The staple news in the *Daily Mirror* and *News of the World* is about sport of the kind most men have played and watch and gamble on. Second to football and racing comes the human-drama section: court reports, accidents and disasters, breakdowns of 'law and order' – including strikes.

The *Evening Standard* likes to boast that its readers are more wealthy than those of the *Evening News*. It prints, as a news item, the fact that the *Financial Times* has bought a full-page advertisement in the *Standard*'s columns, thus proving the existence of big investors, men of distinction, among the readers. Quality news must accompany quality advertisements. Here is an example (16 September 1969 again). The gossip column, 'Londoner's Diary', describes a wealthy publisher's party, informing us that the Chairman of British Steel was present, dressed as an Arab oil salesman, together with the Keeper of the National Portrait Gallery, in 'sashed and muffled furbelows as a Beardsley interpretation of the Prince Regent', and Bernard Levin as Bernard Levin. The piece continues: 'it was a pity that some of the sparkle [*!*] had not spread to the Savoy for the dinner given in honour of J. B. Priestley's 75th birthday.' The Londoner supposes that Priestley must have been dissatisfied with his company, distinguished fellow-writers, some senior, some junior (Richard Church, Iris Murdoch, Angus Wilson): 'Is that really the best that can be done to honour a writer whose characteristics may not endear him to everyone ...?' (To be sure, Priestley might have enjoyed the additional 'sparkle' of a few dancing-girls but, surely, not Lord Melchett in a fez.) My point is, though, that the Londoner's gauche attempt to pose as an arbiter of elegance, this vulgar self-parody of snobbish knowingness, is meant as news – news of the quality, for the quality, of no interest to the man searching the general vacancies column of the popular *Evening News*.

We must remember that scores of local reporters and stringers all over the country are helping to maintain the personality of the national newspaper, by supplying it with the kind of news it usually prints, in the style it usually prefers. When I worked as a reporter on the *Oxford Mail*, in 1957, we all knew which newspapers would want which of our local specialities. For instance: gossip about smart-set undergraduates (some London papers wanted only the titled students); reports of arcane sports (like college bumping-races); industrial disputes in the Cowley motorworks; scholarly and scientific discoveries; petty squabbles and intrigues of university teachers; long reports of sex-crime trials. Twelve years later, the London papers have scarcely changed. I could follow precisely the same routine tomorrow.

Let us return to 16 September, when the *Standard* chose to lead with a President's speech, on the ground that quality readers would be impressed by his speech-writer's devious musings, whereas the *News* told of an English mountaineer and his eight-year-old son, apparently killed while climbing the Matterhorn. The *News* began: ' "No hope" for Britons on Matterhorn – "Ridiculous to take child of eight up there" '. The feature article on page 10 is headed: 'David Wainwright and Frankie McGowan put the question. How much of a daredevil can you let a child be?' The *Daily Mail* of 18 September led with the same story (it was a cliffhanger, lasting several days: I use the term without callous intent) and the reporter referred to the dead man as 'the foolhardy Mr Clarkson, ignoring warnings'. On page six we have the inevitable feature entitled 'How far should a father push his son?' by Lynda Lee-Potter: 'I know that the climbing Clarksons are an extreme case but, in fact, don't we all nowadays tend to push our children to the limits?' She sounds like a clergyman preaching a sermon. 'Don't you sometimes . . .? I know *I* do.' A good deal of newspaper work consists of preaching sermons, making moral noises; and the news items are often selected to illustrate the sermon.

Although the *Daily Mail* is intended for a rather wealthier readership than the *Evening News*, the two newspapers have much in common, illustrated by their treatment of the Matterhorn deaths. Both are published by Associated Newspapers Ltd, from Carmelite House; they are consistent supporters of the Conservative Party; they employ a winsome lady journalist to write in a bright ladylike way about aspects of the week's news, with thoughts about the difficulties of family life, dinner parties and *au pairs*; each has another columnist, a TV personality (the *Mail* has Bernard Levin, the *News* has Lord Arran, a director of the newspaper) and both these write in a 'forthright', 'outrageous' style about the week's news, concentrating on the wrongfulness of foreigners, Communists and the Labour Government. The personality these papers wish to present is that of a motorized family in a residential suburb, with motto: 'Safety first'. Levin and Arran are intended as a kind of eccentric Daddy: he gets a little cross sometimes, but he doesn't really mean all the nasty things he says; mother knows what's best; be kind to animals, look after the old folks and be careful crossing the road. Always do what the doctor orders; and the teacher, and the policeman, and the judge. This is the pattern of living endorsed (and, often, enjoyed) by *Mail* sub-editors; these men arrange the news to fit in with these preconceptions.

The tendentious news items and little sermons about 'foolhardy Mr Clarkson' are characteristic of newspaper admonishments. We are all miserable sinners, but the only organization anxious to tell us so is the British press. Whether Mr Clarkson was foolhardy or not, the *Mail* was bound to admonish him. Readers are admonished too. Sometimes the press suspects its readers of dangerous thoughts, resentment of authority – when, for instance, a judge sentences a 'spy' or a thief to 30 years imprisonment while more hated law-breakers get off more lightly. The press does not reflect these sentiments: it instructs us not to be sentimental.

Here is an example of the censorious tone adopted. The *Mail* offers a brief news report about some squatters who have taken over an empty 60-room mansion in Piccadilly; but the comment (front-page) is three times as long: 'No doubt the squatters hope to gain public sympathy by cocking a snook at authority. Already they are spouting the usual stuff . . . We are supposed to be angered by the fact that some flats and offices stay empty for a long time. But do the squatters' leaders really imagine that temporary gimmicks can do anything to solve the housing problem? . . . These lotus-eaters . . . We are fed up with anarchists hawking their consciences round other people's property.' The *News* offers a similar treatment, a brief report, a longer comment ('Some of these hippies come from abroad. Let them drop out of Britain . . .') and a full-page picture-feature designed to denigrate the squatters and make their name stink. 'Some sleeping-bags contain one body; others peacefully sleeping couples. It smells *dirty* . . .' Reference to toilet facilities and excreta is freely made; the *Sunday Telegraph* follows this line, alleging in a leader that the squatters have not been properly 'house-trained'. (Query: when smearing, why does the press prefer 'house-trained' to 'pot-trained'?)

Readers will have different views about the merits and failings of these squatters, if they happen to meet any of them. But, as readers, we know in advance that the *Mail* and the *News* will call them dirty and try to make their name stink. In any strike, how-ever justified (and every newspaper will admit that *some* strikes are justified – only not the one that is being reported just now), we know that the *Mail* and the *News* will not be supporting the strikers. The line is laid down in the opinion columns and thd news is reported and sub-edited to match. My great-uncle worked

as a sub on the *Mail* during an important pre-war transport strike;
he was a Labour supporter in private life, so he locked up his car
in case it was commandeered by strike-breakers, and then he
walked to work in the *Mail* offices, sub-editing the predictable
anti-strike copy. Things have not changed much since then. Not
only is there no national newspaper willing to support the Labour
Party; there is none (with the exception of the small-circulation
Communist paper, *Morning Star*) which will report and sub-
edit news of a strike without a strong bias to the employers'
side.

In my 16 September *Mail* I find a report, interlarded with
comment, about a proposal by Liverpool employees to take over
three GEC-English Electric plants which their employers had
decided to close: other employees demonstrated against this
plan, yelling anti-Communist slogans like 'GEC, not USSR', and
'Go home, you bums'. It was predictable that the *Mail* would
take the side of the noisy ones. The report is headed: '*Workers
beat factory rebels*', and goes on: 'It was the biggest snub yet for
the Workers Control Movement, largely run by university
academics, who advised the shop stewards on how to occupy the
factories in protest against a decision to make 3,000 workers
redundant.' The story behind this extraordinarily ambitious plan,
by the Joint Action Committee of shop stewards, would make an
interesting human drama, would it not? But the press does not
want to give it to us. It wants to fight these men and frustrate
their attempt to safeguard their comrades' livelihoods.

The only truly national journals in which industrial action is
efficiently reported as news are minority papers, like the *Financial
Times* and *The Economist*, designed to be read by investors and
the upper levels of management. Such readers want to know the
facts about a dispute in another part of the country, and they
get them straight without anti-striker distortion: they do not
need the pro-employer bias, since they are on the side of the
employer already. Other quality papers sometimes offer news of
industrial disputes without grotesque distortion and selection of
facts, more as a matter of general interest, particularly on the
business pages. But the popular papers, those designed for
working-class consumers, are almost invariably vehement against
strikers, mingling comment with reporting, coaxing the strikers
back to work, blackening their cause in the eyes of other workers.

Reporters are quite often Labour supporters and sometimes active
trade unionists. But to stay in the profession under these circum-

stances, it is necessary to be an unusual kind of person – exceptionally obedient to authority. It is much easier to do the job if one has a natural respect for established authority. In an industrial dispute, the reporter gets his information from the employers' PR man; in a demonstration, he stands beside the policeman. It is, of course, often hard to get into a strike meeting, or to make contact with a shop steward or a works convenor: they are not always on the telephone at home, and are still harder to contact in the factory. But the employers often have a pleasant spokesman with a bottle of sherry ready for journalists. The ideal labour correspondent or industrial correspondent is a man who is genuinely Conservative and believes his views to be moderate. He must also be able to be friendly with people on the other side, and act as a spy if necessary. During the Piccadilly squatters story, mentioned above, many newspapers were able to send in a young reporter disguised to look like a squatter type.

People are afraid of the national press. Its tendency to expose, pillory and persecute the weakest citizens means that the arrival of London journalists can have something of the menace of a secret policeman! A leading reporter on one national journal, a paper concentrating on vehement 'exposures' of petty offenders, became a partner in a private detective agency which also dealt in evicting tenants from landlords' property. When this paper was reported to the Press Council for allegedly libelling a homeless man, their reporter's agency was engaged to investigate the man's character. His petty court convictions were listed, and an account was typed out of the insanitary conditions in which he and his family had lived, in overcrowded accommodation. When I took an interest in this man's case, these documents were shown to me, at the newspaper's head office, so that I would be prejudiced against him for not being properly 'house-trained'.

We might note that people are not so afraid of *local* reporters. The young reporter may feel embarrassed at intruding on private grief, for instance when calling on relatives of victims of a fatal accident; but he often finds himself welcomed, since relatives want their dead commemorated, attention to be finally paid; they want their bereavement to 'make news' as a kind of ceremony. Local papers are organized in 'chains' which are even more consistently Conservative in bias than the nationals; but the editors and managers are unwilling to offend neighbours deeply ('After all, we have to *live* here') and they are far less guilty of persecuting and pillorying.

Conscientious journalists who believe in what they are doing sometimes worry about their responsibility. Here are two, one a Labour parliamentary candidate, the other a Conservative councillor and parliamentary candidate. The first, Keith Kyle, wrote in the *Listener* (4 September) about the BBC's responsibility during the fighting in Northern Ireland. It was necessary to exclude 'incendiary persons such as the Rev Ian Paisley and Miss Bernadette Devlin' from the screen: these counted as 'extremists'. The press, followed here by the BBC, had decided that the M.P., a leader of the Civil Rights campaign on behalf of the Roman Catholic minority, counted as an extremist, to be bracketed with Ian Paisley as her opposite number. We will return to this.

Kyle claims that, for a journalist, 'the definition of responsibility includes the regarding of a violent breakdown of law and order as something approaching the ultimate ill'. This is a very important admission. That is exactly the principle on which most journalists work – when reporting events in this country. (Exactly the opposite may be the case when reporting events in a Communist country, like Czechoslovakia.)

Timothy Raison, the Conservative, comments (*Evening Standard*, 16 September) sympathetically on Kyle's plea for self-censorship, his proposal 'to underplay events in an attempt to calm passions and be responsible'. He adds that this is particularly important with television and photographs, since 'the camera tends to come out on the side of the underdog and against authority. I suspect that the Left has always won more support through visual appeal than through verbal arguments.' This is a poor argument, since it is always possible to print photographs of policemen looking like underdogs – wounded or being outnumbered in a scuffle – and such photographs are normally chosen to illustrate news of clashes between British police and others. More important is Raison's suggestion that it is necessary for the press to censor itself in order to avoid creating public sympathy for the Left, for the underdog up against authority.

Authority must be presented as 'moderate': thus two 'extremists' must be found. The press coverage of the Northern Ireland troubles has followed the pattern for reporting Rhodesia's steady transformation into a breakaway republic, with an apartheid basis. The man in charge is a right-wing conservative, and there are grounds for complaint against his authoritarian and repressive measures. Nevertheless, he must be supported, since he represents law and order, and he has promised liberal reforms: Whitehead is

the moderate, Winston Field is a right-wing extremist, Nkomo
in jail is a left-wing extremist. As the right-wing extremists
succeed each other, they become in turn forces of law and order,
moderates flanked by hawks and doves – and the left-wing
extremist is still in jail. So it has proved in Northern Ireland.
Right-wing Captain O'Neill passed on his 'moderate' image
(between Devlin and Paisley) to the more right-wing Chichester-
Clark, who may yet pass it on to the still more right-wing Craig;
and the British press will still regard the new man as a force of
law and order (between extremists Devlin and Paisley). In terms
of lay-out: the Cameron Report on Northern Ireland criticized
the Civil Rights Movement, the anti-Catholic fanatics and the
former Home Secretary, Craig – among others. The *Evening
Standard* chose these three to ask their comments, and printed
their three photographs, with Craig firmly in the centre. But the
word 'moderate' ought not to be taken to mean 'middle', still less
to mean the forces of law and order.

An example of how a layout can destroy or distort an article
commissioned from a journalist whose policy runs counter to the
newspaper's: The *News of the World* (10 August) printed an
article by C. H. Rolph, the law reformer, about recent Home
Office Criminal Statistics, dealing with Offences Against the
Person. Rolph poured cold water on scare headlines like 'Crimes
of Violence Up' – explaining, for instance, that the statistics
included offences like abortion and sending threatening letters.
But the *News of the World* printed the cool, thoughtful piece under
scare headlines: 'CRIME INC. Why violence is now showing a
shocking increase in Britain.' The photograph illustrating the
article showed a bowler-hatted man (the underdog) being coshed
by a masked man; the caption read: 'This robbery was staged,
but every day, more victims fall under the cosh of a thug.' The
cross-headings to the article were these: Murder, Assault, Threats,
Gangs.

The *News of the World* is in favour of severe retribution for
convicted criminals, and used even Rolph's liberal article to
spread this doctrine. Other doctrines which the *News of the World*
filters through its news pages include the need to restore capital
punishment (assisted by a ballot for readers) and the need to
restrict further immigration (assisted by tendentious feature-
stories about coloured people in Britain, and selected court
reports). The message of the *News of the World* is 'Be normal.
Work hard, play hard, lead a law-abiding family life. Criminals,

foreigners and coloured immigrants shall be your scapegoats.'

Lord Wigg has remarked on the press's tendency towards 'scapegoatism'. The newspapers represent the voice of authority, an authority more repressive and condemnatory than clergy, teachers or government. One Sunday in January 1969, the seven London national papers exposed and condemned the following: students, drug-takers, strikers and sex-maniacs; lazy bus-drivers, a union's accident-claim policy, bad craftsmanship, wealthy tenants, pilfering in Clydeside shipyards, working-class drag shows, an alleged swindler ('Deport this man . . . an alien born in Poland'), and Professor Eysenck's questionnaire on sexual attitudes. Such people are easy to hit. Lord Wigg noted that foreigners and racial minorities were the easiest targets for newspapers which wished to appear forthright and hard-hitting.

Politicians know this. Mr Enoch Powell became an important political figure in the newspapers, and thus in the mind of the nation, because his generalizations about racial minorities were considered newsworthy and printed at great length. Newspapers complain when Mr Powell is shouted down at public meetings, holding that this is an infringement of his freedom of speech; but this problem would not be so serious if the press had not chosen to give Mr Powell's remarks so much publicity. His freedom of speech has been enormously enlarged. Every journal wants him to write articles for them; every speech is publicized. His views are not effectively countered. When his leader, Edward Heath, expressed opinions on immigration not dissimilar from Mr Powell's, the Sunday papers reported the event, with front-page photographs and headlines like the *Mirror*'s 'The Day Enoch Smiled'. Only two Sundays offered a comment, the *Sunday Telegraph* and the *News of the World*, both commending the Heath-Powell rapprochement. More recently, Mr Powell has suggested that Irish citizens should be treated as foreigners – another interesting news item. But you would think that journalists would want to find out why Mr Powell made this suggestion; whether, for instance, it is true that Irishmen are more unpopular in his Midlands constituency than they are elsewhere in England.

Foreigners can always be criticized – even their forces of law and order. But the main international loyalty of the British press is to the United States alliance. News of America overshadows all other foreign news. Other subjects of importance are the struggle against communism, and the remains of Britain's empire and its successor-states. Even wars and revolutions get little coverage from London papers unless they can be fitted into one of these frameworks. Latin America is not news except for Cuba (communism, America's enemy); Guyana was news (ex-British empire, communist menace) when Dr Jagan was premier, more newsworthy than the rest of Latin America put together; and, for the same reason, Ghana under Dr Nkrumah was more newsworthy than the rest of West Africa – the unknown Chad and Niger Republics, for instance. Political prisoners and literary censorship in Latin America or, say, Thailand or Persia or Portugal – these matters are not newsworthy; but any such occurrence in a communist country is very newsworthy indeed. Of course, much foreign news *can be found* in newspapers like *The Times* and the *Daily Telegraph*; but it is rare to find it displayed and made into an important issue unless it relates to one of these three: United States, anti-communism, ex-Empire.

Readers of the quality newspapers may be satisfied with the product: at least they are treated as equals. Readers of the popular newspapers have no reason to be satisfied: they are being talked down to, got at, coaxed and bullied. The question in the producer's mind is not 'What shall I tell them? What do they want to know?' It is: 'What will be the effect on them if I tell them this, or this? How can I make them work harder, stop striking, respect the judge's decision, vote Conservative?' Journalists commenting on the press generally concentrate on the qualities, which they read themselves, and merely laugh at the populars: 'Nobody reads *The People*,' said a *People* journalist. But these popular papers are an important part of the nation's political, imaginative and intellectual life. Plenty of workingmen will claim that they are uninfluenced by the papers they read (chosen purely for amusement, sports news, jokes), but they must be affected in their judgment of affairs by a steady consistent drip throughout the paper, preaching conformity, xenophobic patriotism and respect for conservative authority; hostility to government and municipal and civil service 'interference', and to dissentients and libertarians of the left.

This oligopoly of large circulation papers has the characteristics of more modern media, like commercial radio and commercial television. An imaginary ideal reader is kept in mind (contemptuously labelled 'the man in the back streets of Derby' – or wherever the London editor comes from) and this image is considered as the lowest common denominator; no commercialist ever thinks of the highest common factor, as Reith's BBC did. When commercial television was introduced, a controlling body was set up, the Independent Television Authority, in the hope of maintaining something like BBC standards. That was because it was new, and everyone recognized the power over men's minds which the controllers of TV would otherwise possess; because the power of the mass-circulation press has grown up over so many years and seems such an ancient institution, no one has been willing to propose an Independent Press Authority, to compel newspapers to present news without the automatic Conservative bias. Still less imaginable is the possibility of setting up a British Press Corporation, government-subsidized, on the lines of the BBC. Yet this could safeguard the quality papers, so vulnerable nowadays, papers which the ruling class, after all, values.

But how could such a change of structure come about? The newspaper proprietors are in an admirable position to prevent such an argument from getting a fair hearing: there would be no forum for debate, merely tendentious news-items attacking those who want to restrict the press-lords' 'freedom'. When the Labour Party Conference discusses the press, the debate is held in secret session, and the party leaders fervently oppose Government interference; they would rather criticize the BBC. During the war years, that famous libertarian, George Orwell, asserted in *Tribune* that the mass-circulation press should be nationalized; in that time of upheaval, Orwell's suggestion was just about practicable. Not so now.

Left-wing and libertarian workers in the media believe in the possibilities of workers' control; but the kind of workers we have, at present, do not want any such thing, will not support it and, if it were imposed upon them, would maintain the media's conservative bias. My more moderate proposal, for a BPC and IPA, following the accepted precedent of broadcasting, would result in the acknowledgment of the principle that the tendencies of both main political parties should be represented in the press. A small step; but a public body is responsible to the public as a commercial organization is not. Further, a new kind of journalist would enter the profession, more responsive to the concept of democratic control, by producers and consumers.

What have these pipe-dreams got to do with 'news'? Simply this: they are unprintable in the newspapers, our main information service, except in a column for cranks, headed 'The Voice of Protest' or 'The Provocative Voice'.

I have suggested that the British press is an enemy of reform, that its news items are reported, selected and presented editorially in such a way as to act as a repressive force. An anti-authoritarian pose is often struck; this is done by scapegoatism – fierce attacks upon public institutions and upon libertarian and equalitarian organizations (like trade unions), or crucifixion of favoured authorities when they fall from grace. When a millionaire or a policeman is brought down, the press kicks.

Reporters will say: 'We just get a good story.' But they get the story they know their editor wants, which he knows his proprietor and the advertisers want; and the reporters have been selected and trained to get that kind of story. Consider this story: an employer sacks a factory worker for having long hair; he does this hoping to please a business associate from Sweden; fellow-workers in Corby (mostly crop-headed Scots immigrants) call a strike. This is a good human-interest story, surely? But it is in fact presented not as a defence of individual liberty, not as an example of management failure – but as a boring story of irresponsible workers threatening 'the nation's' economy. Strikes are full of good stories, but they are not used. Tragedy: a cured drug addict dies after taking medicine prescribed by a doctor, and a small amount of whisky. The *Evening Standard* made a report of the inquest the front-page lead; but it did not mention (25 July) the cause of the man's death until the bottom of the back page. The story was about the ex-addict's past history and the drugs of which he did *not* die. 'A coroner hears ex-addict's story of town where they start on cannabis. "DRUG HELL" OF WELWYN GARDEN. "A coffee bar – the place to buy them".' Without careful examination, it was hard to tell that the man had been cured of his addiction and had died from licit and prescribed drugs. Cannabis is the villain of the piece – though who has died of cannabis? The story begins: 'An ex-drug addict said today he became "hooked" after starting on cannabis . . .' The reason for this is that there is a move to legalize cannabis, and the weight of the press is inevitably thrown towards the support and maintenance of restrictive regulations, known as 'law and order'. The story about whisky and doctor's prescriptions is not the story they want.

It is wrong to blame the reporter for the state of the press, as it is wrong to blame the policeman for the state of the law: that is scapegoatism. Martin Jude, treasurer of the Miners' Association, put up this defence for a local industrial correspondent 130 years ago: 'As the poor gentleman has to please his masters to obtain a little bread for his wife and family, it is impossible for him to refrain from following the occupation he was hired for, viz. that of throwing cold water on any movements of the working classes to better their conditions.'

4

Anatomy of a crisis

TOM BAISTOW

If the story of Fleet Street had to be summed up in one of its own alliterative, oversimplifying headlines, it would read something like 'PRESS PARADOX: SUCCESS SPELLS CRISIS'. For although the British buy more newspapers, proportionately, than anyone else except perhaps the Swedes – 48 people out of every 100 take one[1] (almost double the readership figure in France) – yet today five out of the eight main national dailies are operating at a loss or barely breaking even, one (the *Sun*) has recently been narrowly saved from death, and the threat of near-monopoly, with its disturbing implications for our kind of society, looms ever nearer.

The factors behind the paradox are manifold and complex, but at the root of the press's malaise lies one simple if uncomfortable truth: we British like our news but we like it cheap, as we do our food. In the case of the press, it is the advertiser who pays the 'subsidy': the average popular paper gets – or rather, these days, hopes to get – 40 per cent of its income from advertising, while the quality paper is even more dependent on this source of revenue – a massive 70 per cent or more. In short, if the 6*d*. paper carried no advertisements it would cost the reader at least 9*d*. and a quality costing 8*d*. or 1*s*. 3*d*. at present would rise astronomically to between 2*s*. and 3*s*. 4*d*. But, although historically we are so addicted to newspaper reading, even a penny rise sends us to the newsagent to cancel the *Daily X* – sometimes only temporarily, but enough of us do it to make price rises a traumatic

[1] Unesco Statistical Yearbook, 1968

D

experience for all newspapers, however successful. (The most dramatic illustration of this phenomenon was provided by the *Daily Mail*: in 1964 when newspapers generally put up their price to 4*d.* the *Mail* decided, against the advice of its then editor, Mike Randall, to hold on at 3*d.*, although this meant forfeiting over £1 million in extra revenue. The short-term effect was a modest rise in circulation, but when the paper's price was raised to 4*d.* just over a year later its sales fell disastrously and Randall was sacked – an episode I will return to later, for it is symptomatic of the populars' instability.) It is axiomatic, therefore, that newspapers undertake price rises only when they are hard pressed, if not desperate. And several of them have been very hard pressed financially since the national stop–go cycle of the earlier part of the decade mushroomed into a full-scale and seemingly endless economic squeeze in 1966. That year the press's own inquiry into its crisis, a survey by the Economist Intelligence Unit,[1] revealed the full extent of the trouble in a devastating and dismaying diagnosis of Fleet Street's deep-seated sickness. For the first time the partly sophisticated yet strangely nineteenth-century structure of the industry was exposed to the cold light of modern business standards, and the verdict was scathing. Among other things, the survey found that:

[The industry's] most striking feature, and possibly its greatest problem, is its dominance by a small number of highly individual proprietors with their own personal interests and philosophy of management . . . The quality of management is uneven and the industry is short of professionally trained managers . . .

There is an urgent need for more detailed budgetary and cost-control schemes . . . The natural respect for editorial freedom has, in some areas, been allowed to overshadow business principles . . .

[The industry is] almost unique in the degree to which control of labour is in the hands of the unions . . . Branch officials have little influence in the operation of the chapels [office-level union section]

[Many production departments are] heavily overmanned... Manning standards are usually set by horse-trading and often bear little relationship to the needs of the job . . . The

---

[1] *The National Newspaper Industry: a survey* 1966.

present wages structure is a jungle and the basic wage bears
no relationship to the take-home pay . . . Drunkenness was
such as would never be tolerated in other industries . . .

Publicity expenditure for the industry is running at a rate
of about £5 million a year but sharp changes in publicity
expenditure have little or no effect on the circulation trend

The value of the emphasis which is placed on exclusivity
and late news is questionable

To understand what has brought this state of affairs about, one
has to go back to the end of the 19th century. On 4 May 1896 a
young journalist named Alfred Harmsworth produced the first
issue of his new *Daily Mail* and changed not merely the face of
British journalism but the structure of the industry itself. When
that first copy of the *Mail* appeared there were already 28 dailies
printing in London alone, most of them, except for *The Times*,
with circulations of a few thousands, mainly in the metropolis,
while another 150 throughout the rest of the country catered for
regional readers. Most cost 1*d*., although *The Times*, easily the
most prestigious of them all, charged 3*d*. – the equivalent of
about 2*s*. in present-day purchasing power. Until that time the
daily paper was a minority habit – only about 16 per cent of the
public bought one – for they were serious affairs by today's
standards, mostly full of 'hard' news, solid accounts of public
events, political and business reports and long leading articles
that had little meaning or appeal for the ordinary working man.
But Victorian technological genius and the need for a basically
literate work force to meet its increasingly more sophisticated
demands provided all the elements for a revolution in Fleet
Street: a network of railways that reached into the most remote
corners of the country, a telegraph system that linked almost
every village with London, and millions of new 'graduates' of the
1870 Education Act, hungry for something to read but for whom
the established press was too dull to warrant the expenditure of a
penny – that, after all, was the price of a pint of Whitbread's
porter.

The hour calls forth the man: Harmsworth (later to be Lord
Northcliffe) was the man who saw the potential market. For ½*d*.
he offered entertainment rather than indigestible information,
news in a palatable form, women's interest stories and features
and the chance to win money in competitions. That first issue
sold nearly 400,000 copies – almost as many as the combined

circulation of the other twenty-eight dailies. The then Lord Salisbury contemptuously dismissed it as 'a paper written by office boys for office boys', but Harmsworth had hit on the formula – a key word I'll come back to – that was to turn serious journalism into a minority taste. Four years later he started to print the paper's Scottish and Northern editions in Manchester and sales soared to nearly a million – a fabulous figure in those days and still a large and profitable circulation in any country outside Britain. The cheap *national* paper had arrived. Today Britain is still the only country with a wide selection of truly national papers that are read the same morning by everyone from the City tycoon to the Yorkshire millworker or the Highland crofter. It is this uniqueness that is both the strength and the weakness of the British national press. Northcliffe reversed the whole pattern of newspaper development as it existed in this country and as it still exists more or less in comparable countries like France, Germany and the United States. Here the nine national dailies sell 15 million copies a day compared with the provincial papers' sales of only 8 million; in France the position is exactly the opposite – the Paris-based dailies sell only 2·4 million compared with the 7 million sold by the regional press.

The immediate and highly profitable success of Northcliffe's innovations naturally inspired imitators and eventually led to cut-throat competition on a scale unknown in other countries; it was this battle for readers in every part of the country that transformed both journalism and the economics of the industry even further. Initially Northcliffe was able to undercut his rivals by $\frac{1}{2}d$. because he introduced the latest time-saving machines such as the linotype (still very much with us, despite its outmoded principle) that cut traditional costs by nearly a half. But he also saw the tremendous potentiality of advertising and offered the new expanding manufacturers like Cadbury and Pears the mass publicity their mass production needed by aiming much of the *Mail* at the housewife, the biggest spender in the ordinary family. In this perceptive exploitation of the reader as *consumer*, profitable though it was to be for half a century, lay the germs of Fleet Street's future sickness. For the battle for mass circulation meant that papers had to continue to sell cheap, even when costs rose – the price of the popular stayed at $1d$. for over forty years – and this in turn led to a more and more intensive drive for advertising revenue to subsidize the retail price.

Journalistically, the most far-reaching effect of Northcliffe's revolution was that it put an end to the classical role of the editor in all but a tiny handful of quality and regional papers. Until then papers had been edited by men of strong political and social convictions who sought to influence public opinion. But Northcliffe was out to make money – originally, anyway. As Kennedy Jones, his collaborator in the creation of the *Mail*, put it candidly to Lord Morley, the statesman who had himself been a journalist: 'You left journalism a profession – we made it a branch of commerce.' By the 1930s the tycoons had taken over completely and their editors were little more than technicians: circulation rather than influence had become the dominant factor, and genuine editorial independence disappeared from all but a handful of papers like *The Times* and *Manchester Guardian*. This was the tragi-comic era of the great circulation war when, in their desperation to win the lion's share of the market, the *Express*, *Herald* and *Mail* in particular offered everything from clothes wringers and copies of Dickens and Shakespeare to free insurance to those who became 'registered readers' – i.e. contracted to place a regular order for the paper. It was during this mad and debasing scramble that the late Lord Beaverbrook's undoubted if dubious genius imposed on British popular journalism a technically slick and superficially brilliant, but basically shallow and often dishonest, pattern whose success in sales terms led his competitors down the same slippery path.

Although Northcliffe pioneered the technique of selling readers entertainment rather than information, it was Beaverbrook who perfected it, if that is the word, in the *Express*, with a cynical mixture of escapism, sensationalism and blatant propaganda (originally in support of his zany but harmless Empire Free Trade campaign, but later malevolently and effectively against Attlee's post-war Labour government). Beaverbrook, like Northcliffe, was the real editor, and Arthur Christiansen, for thirty years the nominal editor, in fact a talented technician who devised the bold typographical presentation and highly developed system of synthesizing news and features, and elevated the 'human angle' into the dogma that still marks the popular paper of today. Christiansen's credo, as he revealed it in his autobiography, was: 'Make the news exciting, even when it is dull. Make the news palatable by lavish presentation. The *Express* must aim at the viewpoint that is optimistic and provocative.' This professional optimism was aimed as much at the businessman's confidence, and therefore at advertising, as at the ordinary reader, and it enabled the *Express* to carry a bold headline slogan across the front page every day for months until almost the outbreak of war in 1939: the headline assured soothingly, 'There will be no war this year . . .' But however phoney this formula in terms of journalistic ethics it won the *Express* a 4-million circulation when others were struggling between the 1- and 3-million marks and gave it a dominant share of advertising and the highest rate per column inch, the touchstone of commercial success.

It was the Beaverbrook–Christiansen partnership, above all, which widened the already considerable difference in character between the serious and popular papers into a gulf that only now is slowly beginning to narrow again. Although superficially the same in editorial structure, the two are radically different, not simply in the sense that Alastair Hetherington, editor of the *Guardian*, is in complete control of policy where his opposite on a popular has to pay attention to his master's voice; the qualities, following the traditional approach still standard for most news-papers abroad, are *writers'* papers, while the populars are essentially *sub-editors'* papers. To oversimplify, the quality, seeking to inform its readers about the most important developments and trends and to analyse and interpret their significance, accords its reporters and correspondents a status often denied their higher-paid opposites on mass circulation papers: it chooses them for their judgment, their ability to write with individual style and authority and more often than not prints what they write virtually as they write it. Naturally, there are sub-editors on qualities, but they are complementary to the writer – they check, cut for space, write the headlines and 'marry' related reports. On a popular the emphasis is vastly different, not merely in terms of news values, the preference for personalities rather than policies, for overt action rather than issues, for what Tariq Ali wears rather than what he says, but in the whole power structure. If the editor is more technician than journalist in the classic definition, his reporters are more news gatherers than writers. Their copy is the raw material: the sub-editors, traditionally higher paid than reporters on populars, rewrite and 'process' it, combining any 'better', i.e. more sensational or colourful, points from news agencies or stringers, however unverifiable or irrelevant, perhaps completely altering the staff reporter's theme or interpretation in the interests of 'readability'. And, final indignity, the length and prominence of the story, whatever its intrinsic merit, may depend on the demands of the layout, for, as in other consumer industries,

the packaging is regarded as at least as important as the content.
(It is instructive to note at this point that the Prices and Incomes
Board inquiry into newspaper costs in 1967 showed that populars
spend more money to produce very much less editorial material
than the qualities.) The end product of this synthesis had the
bright polished uniform finish of plastic, even if it concealed more
than it revealed about the true world; but like plastic it com-
manded the mass market and handsome profits.

Then in the middle of the 1950s several new factors began to
erode Fleet Street's flamboyant prosperity. The first, although its
full impact was not felt for a few years, was the arrival from the
United States of market research. Until then advertising had
been largely an intuitive affair; obviously, mass circulations were
ideal for selling washing powders, but much of the advertising
was won either by high-powered space-selling teams, a paper's
inherited reputation for 'pull' (Northcliffe's legacy to the *Mail*),
or the advertising director's 'old-boy-network' contacts. The *News
Chronicle*, for example, lured its advertising chief from a rival
in the 1930s and paid him a reputed £10,000 a year (£50,000
today) plus a Rolls Royce, because of his undoubted influence
with the agencies that place advertising. Market research, by analysing readerships and categorizing them in terms of purchasing
power – the A, B, C1, C2, C3, D and E classes – and measuring
the paper's effectiveness in terms of cost per inch per 1,000 readers,
shattered the old mysteries and initiated the changeover which
polarized advertising between, say, the *Mirror* at one (the mass)
end of the spectrum, and the *Financial Times* at the other
(specialist) end, leaving those in the middle, like the *News
Chronicle* (whose celebrated 'pull' was revealed to be a myth)
fighting desperately for what was left. This was bad enough but it
coincided with the end of newsprint rationing. From the start of
the war until 1957 the supply of newsprint had been pegged, and
as this reduced papers to shadows of themselves millions of
readers got into the habit of buying more than one daily. Not
only did this inflate circulations but advertisers had to queue up
to get into any paper because of the limited space. Inevitably,
when in the early 1950s papers started to increase their size again
duplicate readership began to decline, slowly at first, and the gap
between the successful and the weaker papers began to widen –
the *Mirror*, *Express* were now at 4 million while the *Mail*, *News
Chronicle* and *Herald* were either static or losing readers.

The next blow was the introduction of commercial television

in 1955. Its impact on the reading habit is obvious: a drop of 2 million, but this figure tells only part of the story, for during the same period the population rose by almost 5 million. Even more telling, despite the overall increase in the national advertising budget, was the way ITV began to siphon off an increasing share of it and threaten the whole basis of the 'subsidized' price across the counter. In 1956 the press's income from display advertising was £91 million and TV's a mere £12 million. Since then TV's share has rocketed to £143 million while newspapers (including Sundays and provincials) get only £102 million.

What finally plunged the press into the crisis that is still as serious, despite the breather provided by the retail price increase of 1968, was the onset of the stop–go cycle at the start of the 1960s. Even before this the struggle had been too much for the *News Chronicle* and its evening paper, the *Star*, which closed down in 1960 despite circulation figures (1,162,000 and 735,000 respectively) which would have made them prosperous in any other country. Now the squeeze added to the survivors' troubles – when industry is squeezed the first saving it makes is on advertising. The outline of the monopoly which had been so insistently forecast with seeming relish by Mr Cecil King, then chairman of the International Publishing Corporation, suddenly became painfully clear: two-thirds of the morning paper circulation was now in the hands of three groups: on the left, the *Mirror* and the *Herald* (which King had reluctantly acquired in his recent takeover of the Odhams magazine empire) together controlled 26 per cent; on the right the *Mail* and the *Sketch*, owned by Lord Rothermere's Associated Newspapers, had 21 per cent; and the *Express* 18 per cent. Since then, of course, the monopoly threat has sharpened with Lord Thomson's takeover of *The Times*, which he added to his *Sunday Times* and provincial chain in 1966. A far cry from the twenty-eight independent dailies of every political hue and widely diverse appeal of sixty years before.

Alerted at last, the government set up a Royal Commission to examine the economic and financial causes of the press's troubles. It merely confirmed statistically the vicious circle newspapermen knew only too well: advertising goes to the successful papers, whether populars or qualities, that have the right groups of readership classes; the papers with less advertising can afford fewer pages and less comprehensive coverage, which lessens their appeal and drives off more readers. To increase their sales revenue by putting up their retail price unilaterally would merely lose more readers; in fact when rising costs force successful papers like the *Mirror* to act as bell-wether and put up their price even their sales fall temporarily, although they normally soon regain their momentum; while the contrast between the thinness of the weaker papers and the new higher price merely draws attention to the contrast with the fatter rivals. The Royal Commission also revealed the bizarre overmanning (three men doing two men's work on average) and inflated wage levels in mechanical departments which kept production costs unrealistically high. (Overtime is such that London machine men got more than £50 *for one shift* on Sunday papers when Christmas fell at the weekend in 1966.) But despite a wide variety of constructive proposals put forward to lessen the imbalance between advertising and sales revenue – they ranged from advertising levies and quotas to government-provided presses and deficiency subsidies – the Commission, with a fatalistic deference to the sanctity of 'market forces' which owed more to Lewis Carroll than to any realistic insight into the implications, concluded that any government intervention would be an intolerable interference with the freedom of the press – or rather of what would be left of the press – and left Fleet Street to pull itself out of the red by its own frayed bootstraps. At least, however, it urged the proprietors and unions to set up a joint body to consider planning and development in the production field. It was 1964 before the unions, as part of a wage settlement, agreed to a joint board and another year before the board realized it was time for newspapers to stop telling British industry what was wrong with it and start investigating its own shortcomings. It commissioned the Economist Intelligence Unit to conduct a confidential survey of 'all the circumstances of publication and production of national newspapers with the intention of making recommendations which will lead to increased efficiency'. The report was to be confidential, not for publication: it proved to be an explosive document. It was presented to the board at a moment of deep crisis in November 1966, when the national papers were reeling from the advertising famine caused by Mr Callaghan's savage July cut-back. Perhaps symbolically, the story was broken by a quality paper: Peter Jenkins, then industrial correspondent of the *Guardian*, managed to get hold of a copy, and his editor published a summary of it; the board reluctantly released the report in full.

Scathing as it was in its indictment of autocratic but uninspired proprietors, mediocre management, underemployed but

overpaid workers, the report acknowledged, rather naïvely perhaps, that:

> The editorial content of a newspaper is largely responsible
> for the success of that newspaper, and it is obvious that
> great emphasis should be placed on this side of any news-
> paper's activities . . The formula, circulation and type of
> readership appear to be more important than the standard
> of management, although poor management can allow a
> strong position to be eroded. It can be difficult for the
> second or third newspaper in a particular category to be
> profitable under the present cost and revenue structure . . .

In other words, it must first be a *good* paper and secondly an
efficient one – but even then it won't necessarily survive if there
is a bigger, stronger rival of similar, although by no means
identical, appeal which provides the advertiser with the satura-
tion he seeks. Or to put it in its bluntest form, the advertiser
decides which papers you are allowed to read. But before discussing the sombre implications of that last phrase I think it is
important to try to analyse the ingredients of editorial success. It
is significant that all the outstanding papers have in effect been
one-man bands in the sense that they were largely the product of
one man's inspiration and conviction. If it is true that no memor-
able poem has ever been written by a committee, it is equally
demonstrable that no paper of any distinction was ever master-
minded by a board.

The tycoons who reduced the editor's status to that of technical
major domo themselves took over the editor's role and power –
whether Northcliffe, Beaverbrook, Camrose of the *Telegraph*, or
Bartholomew of the *Mirror* – and each imposed his own idiosyn-
cratic formula and personality on his paper and gave it a momentum which notably in the case of the *Mirror* and the *Telegraph*
has been skilfully maintained by their successors. Superficially,
no two papers could be more disparate in content and style than
these two, but both, before market research had been invented,
were shrewdly aimed at a definable social class or classes with
clear-cut and identifiable tastes and aspirations which also offered
the advertiser obvious advantages. Both formulas have proved
remarkably durable.

The *Telegraph* is a quality more in presentation than in content
(significantly, it has always kept its price below other qualities).
Camrose, who started out as a young journalist in Wales, took

over the *Telegraph* when it was in decline and set out to cater for the emerging suburban middle classes, combining a dignified and sober if dull layout and flavour which satisfied their yearning for respectability and 'status' with a simple editorial style and easily the most comprehensive news coverage – including the longest and most detailed court reports carried by any paper, serious or popular. Camrose, editor-in-chief as well as proprietor, kept tight day-to-day control of the editorial side, reputedly reading every proof of every issue; today his son, Michael Berry (now Lord Hartwell) who succeeded him as editor-in-chief, maintains the tradition, modifying the formula slightly from time to time to adjust to changing tastes, but sticking basically to his father's recipe. It has paid dividends, with the *Telegraph*'s tremendous success in the 'situations vacant' field, although ironically its advertising pull led it into a venture which cut its profitability: the *Sunday Telegraph* was started at the height of the advertising boom to cash in on the queue of advertisers waiting to get into the *Daily Telegraph* and to rationalize its machine costs by printing seven days a week; but the squeeze means it has to be subsidized by the daily. Which underlines once again the unstable nature of advertising as a major prop in the financial structure of the press.

Harry Guy Bartholomew, a rough, semi-literate genius with the common touch in full measure, took the *Mirror* from a shaky 25,000 to 4,300,000 with an equally perceptive formula, outwardly based on the old Sunday paper staple of crumpet, crime and cricket. But behind all the boldly displayed pin-ups and frothy features was an identification with the working man and woman's grievances and desire for a new social deal that was to become a considerable political force during the war and play a major part in preparing the seedbed for Labour's victory in 1945. 'Bart' was always the real editor of the *Mirror*, and when he was unseated by Cecil King in 1951, King, while assuming managerial control, handed over editorial direction not to the then editor but to Hugh Cudlipp, a brilliant exponent of the Bartholomew technique. Under this team of complementary talents, one managerial, the other journalistic, the *Mirror* soared to 5 million: King and Cudlipp subtly modified the Bartholomew formula to take account of better standards of living and taste, but they never lost sight of the basic nature of the paper's appeal. When King himself was sacked in 1967 and Cudlipp took over IPC he became relatively remote from the day-to-day running of the *Mirror*, and its verve suffered. His return to direct editorial control since the Reed takeover of IPC can only augur well for the paper: all the evidence is that the master-mind must be in constant touch with every development on the paper, for each issue must continue to reflect not merely the outline of the formula but the persona which informs it.

There was no greater exponent of day-to-day, even minute-to-minute control of his paper, wherever he was, than Lord Beaverbrook. For years he lived in an apartment in the *Express* building and even in his eighties he maintained a constant flow of dictaphone instructions and criticisms that kept his editors on their toes. Today Beaverbrook and his faithful man Christiansen are dead and the formula which made it the most copied paper not merely in Britain but in the world, the slick sub-editing, the vicarious experience, the synthetic glamour wrapped up in typographical cellophane, is as old-fashioned in the sophisticated, permissive 1970s as the Hollywood whose candy-floss escapism it paralleled in print – as its declining circulation figures show.

If failure to modify a successful formula can erode even a strong paper's foundations, too violent or too frequent changes can destroy it, as in the case of the *News Chronicle*, whose closure in 1960 brought about the 1961–2 Royal Commission into the *economic* causes of the press's problems. For although it was the polarization of advertising which finally finished the *News Chronicle* off, what started the rot was a sudden and unsubtle switch from a liberal, left-wing policy to a narrow right-wing pro-American line in 1949. Under the progressive joint leadership of Lord Leighton, as chairman, and Gerald Barry, as editor – and he was the real editor – the *Chronicle* reached a profitable circulation of 1·6 million and won a considerable reputation for its intelligent journalism and independent viewpoint. When Lawrence Cadbury, of the chocolate family, which owned it, took over the chairmanship and replaced Barry with a weak editor who uncritically accepted his right-wing line, readers began to desert in their thousands. To try to staunch the flow Cadbury attempted to turn the paper into a kind of poor man's *Express* – he was not the only one to make this fatal mistake – and merely drove readers away in hundreds of thousands.

By an appropriate irony, the paper Cadbury sold the *Chronicle* to, the *Mail*, has been suffering on and off from inconsistency of formula since Northcliffe's brother, the late Lord Rothermere, took it over on its founder's death. A depressing measure of this editorial instability is the present Rothermere's concept of the expendability of editors – the current occupant of the *Mail* chair is the seventh since the war (the EIU report, which criticized the *Mail* because 'neither the editorial function nor the accountancy function are separately represented on the executive board', pointed out that 'the proprietor . . . continues to exert great influence throughout the organization, and largely dictates the policy'.) Two of the seven editors, William Hardcastle and his successor, Mike Randall, gave the paper brief injections of a more serious, liberal approach but neither was given the time that every journalist knows is essential for modifying or recreating a paper's formula. In the case of the *Mail* the profits of the diversified parent company, Associated Newspapers, which also owns an extensive provincial chain, provide a financial cushion, but the paper's circulation continues to fall.

The editor-changing routine is an unfailing symptom of the paper which is no longer sure of its *raison d'être* (the *Sun/Herald* have had seven since the war, the *Express* five since Christiansen's 25-year reign ended in 1957); the assumption underlying it is breathtakingly naïve – that the *next* editor will bring instant magic to the circulation problem. After three years and no miracle the board again sets out in search of a new saviour. The ensuing upheaval shakes the staff's morale and confidence, more readers are driven away by sudden and inexplicable changes in policy and format, the falling circulation is reflected in declining advertising, the vicious downward spiral accelerates . . . Even if the new editor *is* a genius, the external and internal power structures of the board-run popular paper are inimical to editorial success. As the EIU report confirmed, the average board is composed of mediocrities who are too afraid or unimaginative to give more than limited authority to the editor. His sovereignty circumscribed, not least when it comes to making fundamental changes in the internal structure of the paper, the new editor, particularly if he has been writer rather than 'sub', has to rely from the beginning on the goodwill and expertise of the 'back bench' – the night, or production, editor and his assistants, who are responsible for the extremely complex job of putting the paper together in a matter of half a dozen hours. Because in the final analysis it is their judgment, their sense of news and other values, their ability to increase or reduce the importance of the stories of the night by the position and treatment they accord them, a strong back bench can soon tame an editor who seeks to introduce new definitions of news or challenge their concept of a good layout. This capacity of back benchers to negative the reforms of an editor with limited power is more serious in its effects than managerial incompetence because the back bench is at the creative heart of a paper, and back benchers are invariably men who have spent their lives sub-editing rather than creating or experiencing events and people at first hand, as reporters do, working at night, out of touch with life as the vast majority of their readers live it – men who learned their difficult and nerve-racking craft, often on the *Express*, in the days when the *Express* was the pace-setting exemplar of success. The back benchers rarely see TV or understand its challenge or its educative influence on readers: they are expert at 'developing' a story arising out of a television programme but their 'copy tasting' reveals daily that they have failed to realize that TV, with its visual immediacy, has usurped the newspaper's role as a reporter of the overt event, whether plane crash or setpiece ceremonial, and that the press must be complementary, exploiting the deeper dimension of the printed word by analysing and interpreting, by digging and exposing.

The increasing demand for a more thoughtful, mature journalism is demonstrated by the evidence of gradual but definite circulation trends: in 1957 the total sale of the populars was 15 million; today it has dropped to 12,494,000; the qualities, which sold only 1,606,000 then, now total 2,267,000. The trend over the same period is even more pronounced in the Sunday field: the populars, which in 1957 sold 25 million, are now down to 21 million; and four of them have closed down – the *Sunday Dispatch, Sunday Graphic, Empire News and Chronicle* and the *Woman's Sunday Mirror*. Undoubtedly the leader of what might be called the counter-revolution, the move back to serious journalism, is the *Sunday Times*, whose success in financial as well as editorial terms may prove catalytic at this critical point in the press's history. Although – or because – his main interest in newspapers is their profit potential, Lord Thomson has the good sense to give his editors complete authority, with the sole proviso that they should not lose money. Given his head, Harold Evans has shown in the *Sunday Times* that there is an expanding market for responsible investigative journalism allied to humane, enlightened attitudes that postulate readers seeking real news. On the other hand, William Rees-Mogg, editor of Thomson's other acquisition, *The Times*, is finding that modifying the formula of such an old-established quality by broadening its appeal is a tricky, expensive and unpredictable operation. The task set Rees-Mogg was to preserve the paper's prestigious if faded image, at the same time to develop its business readership and to attract the young products of the expanding higher-education system, thus raising the static circulation to half a million to begin with – and, not least, winning valuable advertising from the *Financial Times* and the *Daily Telegraph* (thereby reducing the *Telegraph*'s profits and reducing the *Sunday Telegraph*'s threat to the *Sunday Times*). Three years later, having spent £6 million on the transformation, or £30-plus for each new reader, Thomson has still got neither his half-million sales figure nor the advertising necessary to turn his vast investment into a profit. This despite the fact that for two years he held its price at 6*d*. – only 1*d*. more than the populars. When it went up to 8*d*. last year sales fell.

Which brings us back to the dangers inherent in the 'cheap' newspaper. The EIU report predicted the deaths of a further three national dailies – one quality and two populars – within five years if the cost structure remained unchanged. In the Parliamentary debate that followed the report, in February 1967, the flood of pious platitudes about the need for a 'strong and free' press did not obscure the fact that neither the present government nor its possible successor was prepared to intervene and risk charges of trying to influence the newspapers. The tragedy is that it may take the part-fulfilment of the EIU prophecy to expose the dangerous fallacy of the widespread shibboleth enshrined in Mr Edward Heath's: 'I do not believe that newspapers can operate on other than a commercial basis.' The point that politicians – and many newspapermen – fail or refuse to grasp is that the press operates on a 'commercial' basis which applies to no other industry: it is as if, say, motor manufacturers agreed to sell their cars at two-thirds of cost price in return for a subsidy from the oil companies anxious to stimulate petrol consumption – a subsidy that might be cut or disappear overnight in changing market conditions.

Already an unhealthy monopoly exists in the evening paper field – only two cities, London and Glasgow, have more than one evening. If monopoly is to be averted at national level, the whole concept of news, information and editorial comment, the most vital commodity in the functioning of a democracy like ours, as a market product dependent on advertising goodwill will have to be radically revised – admittedly not an easy task in view of the press's own reluctance to discuss the subject and Parliament's unwillingness to take the problem seriously, despite the political implications of a built-in right-wing bias that would be intensified by further closures. Contrary to common belief, new technological developments and the introduction of colour printing are unlikely to revitalize newspapers as a whole: such innovations call for heavy capital investment and would leave the weaker papers at an even greater disadvantage.

Plainly it will take considerable time and a conscious, organized effort to educate the public that it will in the end get the papers it wants only if it is willing to pay more for them, as continental readers already do (the equivalent there for a popular is nearer 9d.; their qualities' price is almost double ours). It is inconceivable that a society which attaches so much importance to free speech cannot in the meantime devise an interim scheme that will reduce the over-dependence on advertising and at the same time make it possible not only for existing papers with big, if 'uneconomic', readerships to survive but for new ones to be established. (Under the present structure the capital cost is prohibitive: Northcliffe needed only £15,000 – Thomson has spent £6 million merely expanding *The Times*.) There is no shortage of ideas, as the evidence to the Royal Commission showed. Only the will is lacking. If we don't generate that among both public and Parliament we shall end up with the press we deserve, but the press no real democracy can afford.

5

The adman cometh

MALCOLM SOUTHAN

A perturbing experience for enthusiasts of the British press was to read the *New Statesman* of 18 July 1969. In that edition, Paul Johnson, editor of what was once *the* radical political weekly in Britain, delivered an article on Israel entitled 'The Militant Peacemaker'. That Johnson wrote with lavish appreciation of Israel should not surprise anyone familiar either with his work or with the recent editorial stance of the *New Statesman*. What was alarming was that bedded amongst the five pages of prose were several advertisements related to Israel, including one for 'Haifa Refineries Limited' and another for that most partisan of companies, Marks and Spencer.

Now, I am assured that the *New Statesman* did not tout for these advertisements on the explicit understanding that the article was to be pro-Israeli. Johnson tells me that occasionally his magazine's advertising department is offered proofs of a long article in advance to help them in their sales campaign, but that those proofs are never shown directly to the advertising company itself. Johnson also assured me that his travelling expenses to and from Israel were paid entirely by the *New Statesman*. Welcome though this information is, it is not enough. Such are the dangers of advertisers dictating views to the press that independence has not only to be preserved, but also to be seen to be preserved.

Whatever the mechanics of the *New Statesman*'s capture of these profitable advertisements, the fact is that the article by Johnson was pro-Israel. A further fact is that some of the advertisers in

E

that issue, for example the Marks and Spencer organization which took a full page ad alongside the article, would have been unlikely to have advertised had the article been anti-Israel. Indeed in view of the fact that Marks and Spencer very rarely advertise in nationally circulated papers and magazines, except when searching for certain grades of staff, it was most surprising that the *New Statesman* received the advertisement at all: had the writer not been Paul Johnson, who has expressed himself in similar vein on the subject of Israel several times before, I doubt whether they would. Certainly they could hardly have been disappointed by the tone of Johnson's article. Whereas the Israelis have, says Johnson, 'on the whole kept their cool', the Arab terrorists have 'paymasters', and attacks by Iraquis are 'senseless'. The Israelis face 'intolerable situations' and do not make the 'mistake of underrating the Egyptian's capacity for self deception'. And 'when pugnacious Arab schoolgirls scream their approbation of the Baghdad hangings to Israel troops', then of course 'acts of savagery will occur'.

To find political writing of this type peppered with advertisements is fortunately still rare in the British press. The same does not, however, apply to commercial copy. The *New Statesman*'s article was simply an adaptation from an unexpected quarter of a time-honoured practice in the British press – aligning advertisements and copy which both deal with the same subject.

There is no cruder illustration of this trick than the so-called advertising feature – articles on themes and about companies which feature in the bordering display advertisements. Who pays for the space taken up by the article? Sometimes the advertiser himself. Sometimes, happy that it is receiving thousands of pounds for the surrounding ads, the newspaper itself shells out.

Because of National Union of Journalists and the Code of Advertising Practice rulings, these advertisement features are usually labelled, more or less prominently, as such. But the dangers of these articles to the newspapers themselves remains. Generally the articles are written in so undistinguished a style and so obviously fawn on the advertiser that it is unlikely that the reader will not sense that the paper is in some way prostituting itself. It goes without saying that a paper which habitually indulges in them is liable to run into a downward spiral – to gain advertisements it is prepared to produce sub-standard articles, but by doing so it loses the reader's respect and ultimately, presumably, his patronage.

Consider the following examples:

Sun, 5 July 1969. 'Merchant navy men who left the sea only ten years ago would scarcely recognize life today in the new generation of supertankers and container ships,' begins an article in praise of the Merchant Navy. 'The day of the over-crowded fo'csle has passed. In most modern merchant ships each crew member has a single berth cabin: officers have private bathrooms as well . . . etc.' Alongside this panegyric, inevitably, lies a display ad, 'Chart Yourself a Career in the Merchant Navy'. Sadly, the writer of the article was Frank Dawes, the *Sun*'s otherwise percipient defence correspondent. Saving grace: the article is headed 'Sun Advertising Special'.

Daily Sketch, 30 June 1969. 'One great enemy of the bikini girl,' goes an article headlined 'It's Time You Shaped Up to Your Bikini', 'is of course her own sweet tooth. Unless that is, you use a sugar free sweetener.' The last paragraph of this homily assures women that even their periods are going to be no problem. 'With products such as Lil-lets you can sun-bathe and swim regardless.' Alongside this mush, a battery of interested advertisers have taken display advertisements, including Sweetex, the firm making sugar-free sweeteners, and Lil-lets themselves, the 'special tampon' manufacturers. Again the saving grace is that the article was properly labelled as an advertising feature. The article was by-lined Carol Hope, said by the *Sketch* to be a 'house name', meaning a name which writers for the *Sketch* use when they wish to hide their own identities.

Daily Mail, 17 July 1969. An article on electronics. 'In electronics, too, British firms are setting the pace . . . and there are reports from many firms of the need for more qualified men.' The piece goes on to praise Elliot Flight Automation Ltd (a member of GEC-Marconi Electronics Ltd). Alongside, Elliot Flight Automation advertise for electrical testers and electrical inspectors. The article is by-lined Charles Darby, a pseudonym for a regular freelance con-tributor to the *Mail*. The paper shuns the saving grace of labelling the piece as an advertising feature.

Such examples, which could be found in virtually unlimited quantities, illustrate one of the crudest methods of advertising pressure. The motoring columns illustrate the more subtle pressures of the advertisers. Some papers, like the *Sunday Times*, allow their motoring correspondents to carry a sting but on other newspapers several writers on cars give no more than sycophantic appreciation. The columnists presumably fear that if they write too harshly, the car firms will withdraw advertisements, and that they, the journalists, will find themselves scapegoats.

In fact it never seems to happen like that, though there was a quaint incident a few months back in the West country when a local garage proprietor withdrew his advertising from the *Bath and Wilts Evening Chronicle* because he did not take to the local man's comparison of the Mini and the Honda. The paper stuck by the writer, and British Leyland, makers of the Mini, appropriately went on record in support of the journalist's right to say what he liked.

Perhaps the classic exercise of the admen's muscles in this country took place in 1961 when members of the Society of West End Theatre Managers, stung by some capsule theatre reviews by one Mr Puff in *The Observer*'s Quick Theatre Guide, withdrew almost all advertisements. *The Observer*, weak at the time because of its editorial stand against the 1956 Suez invasion, fought for several weeks but in the end had to compromise by curbing Mr Puff's activities. (During the battle the *Sunday Times*, *The Observer*'s principal competitor, did not support its rival by also banning theatre advertisers from its columns.)

Papers with a tradition of radical journalism like *The Observer* and the *Guardian*, have often been flamboyantly and inspiringly reckless about the effect of their text on advertisers. But if these two papers are the bravest, the harsh reality is that only the handful which have invulnerable circulations are able to withstand to any degree the erosive effects of the advertisers.

One of the ironies of Fleet Street is that some of the papers which are journalistically the most degenerate – *The People*, the *News of the World* and, in a different way, the *Expresses* – react in the toughest and most correct way to improper advances from the advertiser. *The People*, for example, is ruthless in its exploitation of sex, and tasteless and vulgar as a newspaper. But compare its treatment of that well-worn trick of the advertising agencies, advertising copy laid out to look like newspaper copy, with that of more reputable papers. Occasionally, the reputable ones will allow an advertisement of this type to nestle alongside ordinary editorial without any indication that it is an advertisement, or with that fact acknowledged only in the tiniest print. Not so *The People*. Atop

the heroine, not by any action on her part, but by a sudden extraction of the painful elements. In the wish-fulfilment stories it just quietly adjusts.'

The 'problem' letters provide the other, factual side of the dichotomy: the picture they convey is of unrelieved anxiety and emotional disturbance. Williams feels that the same process operates in the way these are answered in that they also preach the same kind of 'adjustment'. I don't think this is always so: their message seems to be as often as not 'nothing much can be done about these situations' and their solutions merely a more or less cheerful resignation to the *status quo*.

In one recent issue of *Woman's Own*, the same problem – conflict between the parent-child bond and a marriage relationship – appeared both as a fiction situation and as a letter. The short story, 'A Pretty Wonderful Person', resolves the conflict between Bill and his fiancée Sheila over his attachment to his mother, in this way:

As Bill and I had got up to leave, it happened. His arm was round my shoulder and there we were. Us – a solid unit of two . . . And she was not quite sure how to come over and kiss him goodbye when she and I were definitely not on touching terms let alone kissing!

I'd triumphed, and she knew it! From now on I'd be the one to share Bill's life . . .

The letter to Mary Grant, one page further on, is headed: 'I can't live without my daughter's love.' The anonymous writer confesses:

I never liked my daughter's boy-friend from the start, but I managed to keep aloof from him. When they married, I went to live with them and there were constant quarrels between my daughter and me until finally she threw me out of her house. For two years I have suffered horribly because of not seeing her or my little grand-daughter. She passes me by in the street without a word, but I know she loves me and must be suffering too. How can I make it up? I'm separated from my husband and I can't live without my daughter.

Mary Grant's reply tries to take a general view of the difficulty:

Mothers have to separate themselves from their daughters – you must face this. But I do appreciate that this is much more difficult when the break comes suddenly, and with great ill-feeling, instead of gradually over the years from childhood. Surely it's not too late for you to build up such a good life among friends of your own, with absorbing interests, that you can write to your daughter, 'let's be friends', without pinning your whole future and emotional life on her response. When you *can* live happily without her, that's when you'll be able to share a little of each other's lives without drama or quarrels or desperate feelings on either side.

Although this reply is well-intentioned and humane it is fundamentally a dishonest one. It neatly avoids all the issues raised: obviously the wretched mother has no friends; why is she separated from her husband; what did she do that led to her daughter 'throwing her out'? And what is the daughter's husband's position in all this? Problem and 'solution' are totally one-dimensional and so in their way as fictional as the story; thus between the fantasy-reality split there is still further confusion of values.

One must therefore question even the therapeutic value of this form of feature as an emotional outlet; even though women's magazines are often praised for their handling of such problems at all – and in many cases this praise is deserved. Rather than this evasive treatment, one is tempted to recommend that the magazine spend some of its large promotional budget on running a genuine consultancy service which would try to work towards real solutions. And if this is too idealistic and unbusinesslike a proposition, surely even within the terms of reference of a women's magazine it would be preferable and possible to present this very real and common human problem in the form of a properly investigated article, with several such case histories thoroughly examined and expertly commented on.

The nugatory content of so much women's journalism and the need to bring it into closer contact with reality – particularly by more real news coverage – strongly motivated my work on the women's pages of *The Times*. The overall tone of equivocation and ambivalence in women's magazines leads one to doubt their overt editorial intention as mere domestic primers. As such I would have little quarrel with them, and would even approve them for thus trying to make up for the deficiencies in young women's education (and young men's too for that matter) in the practical and emotional skills of home life. Even in its purely domestic function, however, the women's press has its critics.

Evelyne Sullerot, author of *La Presse Feminine*, thinks that women's magazines *create* anxiety in the readers: she refers to what one woman called the 'Elle complex'.

Ann Mallalieu, in a speech made when she was president of the Cambridge Union, succinctly summarized another common argument: 'We treat women as a sub-culture with special magazines and newspaper columns which are invariably filled with domestic trivia; then people turn round and accuse women of being interested in nothing but domestic trivia.' Betty Friedan, in her passionate and persuasive best-seller *The Feminine Mystique* goes much further. The theme of her book is that the women's magazines and their advertisers are linked in an unspoken conspiracy to induce women to abandon their personal sense of identity and identify totally with the housewife role. In a chapter entitled 'The Happy Housewife Heroine' she analyses the change in the American printed media over twenty-five years of the ideal image of woman from independent career girl to suburban mother, and asks 'Why does Occupation Housewife require such insistent glamourising year after year?' An answer to this question is given by Alva Myrdal and Viola Klein in their long and factual study *Women's Two Roles*. The status of the housewife is low, they assert; always 'derived from her husband as a kind of reflected glory, not from the quality of her own work'. They go on:

> To counteract this state of affairs, which many women find depressing, a cult of Homemaking and Motherhood is fostered by press and propaganda. The sentimental glorification which these activities receive may flatter many housewives, but in the long run it does more harm than good, for it encourages them to indulge in an irrational self-pity and prevents them from assessing their situation at its true value.
>
> Sometimes this glorification has a suspicious air of persuasion: as if women needed convincing that their lot is better than they thought. Whether this impression is true or not, the sentimental cult of domestic virtues is the cheapest method at society's disposal of keeping women quiet without seriously considering their grievances or improving their position. It has been successfully used to this day, and has helped to perpetuate some dilemmas of home-making by telling them, on the one hand, that they are devoted to the most sacred duty, while on the other hand, keeping them on the level of unpaid drudgery.

Myrdal and Klein's interpretation of the wider social function of women's magazines is an appealing one – or would be, but for the fact that for many women, marriage and domestic life seem to represent a preferable choice (one might almost say a softer option) to a more independent, socially-involved existence. But if this is so, it should then be asked why the housewife role should demand the massive psychological reinforcement which the women's magazines and most of the women's pages and features in newspapers provide.

Among the more feminist-minded of the critics of the women's press, the view prevails that the conspiracy is a masculine one. The more extreme, such as Friedan, hint at male psychological imbalance: to them the edifice is no more than a monstrously hollow female cult idol, from out of which a small boy's voice calls for a lost and idealized mother love.

That the content of women's journalism is at source determined by men is certainly true. Within the business, the notion is often heard that the women's press has to exist to keep women journalists out of harm's way: one senior and much respected doyenne of the women's pages, when told at the age of nineteen that she was to take over her paper's women's features, burst into tears and told her editor, 'You've ruined my career!'.

As well as being, obviously, owned and published and physically produced by men, some publications also have men editors, including *Woman's Own* and *Nova*. Two of the newspaper features intended primarily for women, those of *The Observer* and the *Sunday Times*, are also edited by men. This may well be a pointer towards their eventual demise. But this unspoken 'conspiracy', if such it is, merely seems to me to be exploiting a need in women themselves.

The increase in numbers and circulations of women's magazines has gone hand in hand with greater freedom for women and more acute and sympathetic perception of their problems over the last fifty years. It could be that the comforting stereotypes, easy role-identification and persistent reification of values of the woman's magazine or feature page are self-generated protective anodynes, masking a deep anxiety among women about their function and identity.

A recent story in *Woman's Own*, appropriately titled 'A Question of Identity', seemed to reflect such an attitude. The heroine Claire is weighed down by her domestic responsibilities: at one point she says to her husband, 'Don't you see, John? I want to do something for myself occasionally. I'm tired of doing things for other people . . .' Later the family plays a game of Who Am I? – and Claire is shattered by their failure to guess that her choice of the letter C is herself.

Her youngest child guesses correctly in the end – but the others protest that the letter should have been M – for Mummy. Her husband comforts her later in bed: 'He isn't used to hearing you called Claire.' 'Neither am I,' she replies. 'Even you – all you call me is darling or luv.' Finally he murmurs to her, 'Sweet Claire, my wilted wild anemone' – her own image of herself. She is satisfied – but is the reader, much less the critic, with a facile resolution like this?

And is society? Perhaps it is the very lack in our collective experience of the cherishing, expressive, biophile, or so-called feminine, values that drives the media to compensate. Or maybe it is, quite simply, that there isn't much else for a woman to do but daydream over a cup of tea, an aspirin and a 'book' when the kids are at school or the old man is round at the pub.

But one further significant factor remains: many of the readers of these magazines are very young – as young as ten or eleven years old, which was when I first started to read them. With *Woman*, *Woman's Own* and *Woman's Realm*, 22 per cent of the readers are between 16 and 24, the biggest single group by seven or eight per cent. This readership pattern among women is repeated among many newspapers, notably the *Daily Mirror* and most of the qualities.

Textbook, sales-vehicle, propaganda machine, confidant, anxiety-maker, anodyne – the women's press is all of these things. It is also for young girls a form of initiation into society's conceptual image of womanhood, a diffused, formalized, symbolic *rite de passage*. As long as society has use for the image it celebrates, it will probably remain, like that image, eternal.

7

Sports page

GEOFFREY NICHOLSON

Despite the apparent national respect for sport, the sports page
has never quite made it socially. Compared with the crack regi-
ments of leader writers, foreign correspondents and critics, sports
writers have been regarded – and sometimes, under protest, have
come to think of themselves – as a kind of journalistic Pioneer
Corps doing an essential job but with cruder, more proletarian
skills. This attitude is more marked in the quality than the
popular papers, and is generally less prevalent than it was a
decade ago. But it persists in subtle forms in most newspaper
offices; and anyway basic damage has been done which will take
some time to repair.

Like other forms of professional snobbery, it is easier to illustrate than to quantify. It shows in various ways: in the limited
prospects which a lot of sports writers see in their careers; in the
lower regard paid to sports page achievements; and in formal
distinctions like excluding sport from that area arbitrarily defined
as News. It has both social and economic explanations. And in the
end it has a certain rough justification. The sports page has come
to live down to its reputation. Largely ignored by proprietors and
editors until it antagonizes readers or runs into libel trouble, sport
has gone its own way, encouraging a strident chauvinism and
triviality at the lower level, and tolerating at the upper a genteel
detachment.

The damaging effect of all this is to discourage intelligent
young recruits to journalism from going into sport, and to under-

mine the established sports writer's respect for the job he is doing. Whatever success he may win on the back page, he feels he has missed the larger prizes. Indeed the very fact of having made a name in sport may turn out to be, because of type-casting, less a stepping-stone than a millstone.

So, while careful to protect his base in sport, he often makes a determined effort to establish a foothold outside. Perhaps in magazine feature writing or broadcasting. This isn't to make extra money or a more negotiable reputation in the trade; not altogether, anyway. These activities reflect the wider interests which he finds he cannot develop through sport. But this needn't be the case. It might be difficult to introduce a reference to eighteenth-century rummers (on which one rugby writer is sufficiently expert to contribute to *The Field*) into a report on Blackheath *v.* Richmond. But otherwise sport, after all, touches on commerce, politics, social and individual behaviour, education, art and craft, and the writer could express himself on all of these if his subject was taken more seriously.

This is not a plea, by the way, for an opening genuflection to Pascal in the lush French manner – simply an acknowledgement that minds as well as muscles are engaged in any game, and that it takes place in a broader context than the field, the dressing room and the directors' box.

It's significant, I think, that so many sports writers who have come to the top in the last six or eight years are equally well-known in other fields—Brian Glanville as a novelist and critic, Michael Parkinson for his television programme on the cinema, Arthur Hopcraft for his book on world famine and his general magazine writing, Christopher Brasher as a television reporter turned executive, Peter Dobereiner (to those who read the small print in the *Radio Times*) as a scriptwriter for satire programmes, and Clement Freud as a storyteller and good food guide. Even Hugh McIlvanney, the most specialized as well as the most accomplished of this group, writes and broadcasts on a variety of non-sporting subjects. And this is not to mention the number of teachers, butchers and personnel officers who come into the press box on a Saturday afternoon.

There is nothing new in this. Neville Cardus has always divided his time between cricket and music, and John Arlott has ranged over poetry, crime, wine, travel and indeed 'Any Questions?' In an intermediate age group there is the poet and publisher, Alan Ross. What is new is the acceleration of the process, and what is

G

significant is that it is peculiar to sport. Could you produce so long a list of political commentators, City experts or fashion writers who have other secondary (or even primary) occupations within journalism?

All the writers mentioned are freelances, or have fairly liberal agreements with their papers. But even staff men employed on the sports page tend to feel a disproportionate sense of achievement if they fill a rather smaller space somewhere in the middle of the paper: one of them, for instance, for his own satisfaction, used to write anonymous music criticism for the *Daily Worker*. I'm not pretending that their motives in any particular instance correspond with those of the disenchanted sports writer I have pictured. But by weight of numbers they make the point that in this country sports writing is not a 'whole' profession.

This is not the case in America. Writing in *Encounter*[1] five years ago, Brian Glanville said: 'British sports journalism is still looking for an idiom; still waiting for its Red Smith, its Damon Runyon, its A. J. Liebling, let alone its Ring Lardner; still waiting for the columnist who can be read by intellectuals without shame and by working men without labour.' To those names could be added George Plimpton, who wrote one fine book about baseball, *Out of My League*, though later accounts of his experiences as a novice thrown to the professional lions of American football and golf have been more mechanical; and *Sports Illustrated*'s Jack Olsen, a variable but witty performer (as he said of the hunting habits of wolves, 'the family that preys together stays together') who has produced one of the most lucid descriptions by a foreigner of the almost untranslatable Tour de France.

The founding fathers who set the tone of British sports writing belonged to the quality press (the popular sports column was a later invention, beginning in the 1930s with Trevor Wignall of the *Daily Express*). The tradition has produced highly admired golf writers like Bernard Darwin and Henry Longhurst, and cricket writers like Cardus and Robertson-Glasgow, but few writers as such. At best they have been stylish essayists, describing with great technical understanding the action as it was staged before them, and occasionally offering a sharp insight or vivid phrase; it was O. L. Owen of *The Times* who coined 'thud and blunder' to describe a really awful rugby match.

Lesser writers from the same school have seemed over-conscious of the need for quality – interpreted as a literary manner which

[1] 'Looking for an Idiom', July 1965.

often conceals the sense. The most conservative element on their papers, they have stuck to archaic forms like L. Hutton – or even Hutton, L. – when all the world knew him as Len, scrummage for scrum, and *lawn* tennis in case some unwary reader should think that they were playing real tennis at Wimbledon. Up to the time of the Thomson takeover, you had to ask for the Sporting Editor and the Sporting Room of *The Times*, and were sharply corrected by the telephone lady if you didn't. Along with this concern for niceties, has gone a general preference for amateur over professional forms of the game, and for old-established fixtures over more exciting new ones (although I have a natural bias towards rugby, which I report, I find it perverse of *The Times* invariably to cover Harlequins' home fixtures, which draw only a few thousand spectators, and not to give priority to the St Luke's *v.* Loughborough College series which, played between future physical training instructors, shows, for better or worse, the way the game is likely to shape through the next generation).

These prejudices have been compounded by an indifference to the mass audience for sport, which needs to be entertained as well as instructed, and by something near contempt for vulgar news values. The traditional heavy sports correspondent is not only sniffy about the reporter who goes round to the dressing room afterwards 'to get the quotes', but suspicious of any digging for background stories. The play's the thing, and you feel that if the stand burnt down, he would refer to it in the final paragraph as an incident which marred an otherwise interesting game.

The heavy men have had the technical ability to discuss sport at a more engrossing level, but have hung back. They have written from the press box. They have not exposed themselves to the kind of experience that enriched Ring Lardner's stories, the intimacy, involvement and constructive boredom of those long train journeys with the Chicago White Sox.

By chance, while I was writing this, a classic statement of the traditional British attitude appeared in *The Times*. U. A. Titley, their rugby correspondent, had been persuaded to contribute a profile of Bob Hiller, the Harlequins and England full-back. It was a good piece, with the personality of Hiller and Titley showing through strongly, but in the course of it Titley mentioned his misgivings about the whole business of interviewing players:

I must confess that I had not looked forward to delving into Hiller's soul, being old-fashioned enough to believe that a critic's honest duty is to tell his readers what *he* thinks, and not what players and officials want him to think. If he is too wrong too often, there is one obvious remedy that his masters can apply.

But is the sports writer only a critic in this narrow, theatrical sense? The point of talking to players and officials is to discover explanations; it's not to adopt their views but to compare them with your own.

Titley belongs recognizably to an old guard nowadays, however, for in the past decade a new generation of sports writers has come to the top on the quality papers: men less attached to amateur concepts, more involved in sport though not with the sporting establishment, more opinionated, more concerned to win readers and closer in their approach to other specialist news reporters. Not that their papers have always greeted them with rapture. Take *The Observer* which, almost in spite of itself, has produced not the most comprehensive but certainly one of the liveliest sports sections in recent years. In 1966 Hugh McIlvanney, the paper's chief sports reporter, won the Hannen Swaffer award for sports writing. In 1969 it went to Christopher Brasher; and the sports page, coupled with the names of McIlvanney, Brasher and Arthur Hopcraft, also took the Granada award. *The Observer*, however, acted as though it was embarrassed rather than pleased with this attention, perhaps feeling that it diverted notice from those qualities by which it set greater store. Little publicity was given to these successes, and if anything sport has lost since then in the allocation of space.

Generally, too, sport has made little progress in either popular or quality papers in winning recognition as News – although most sports coverage is essentially news of the highest topicality. It remains separate and unequal. Papers will lead the front page on business affairs, labour relations, crime (all of them departmental subjects); even fashion is good for a second lead at times. But sport leads only in certain exceptional circumstances; after an overnight world title fight in the early editions of the evening papers, which are basically racing sheets anyway, and in the Saturday classified editions. If it gets on to the front page at all, it is usually as a semi-political or social story: the d'Oliviera affair or the wedding of a footballer. This is not important in terms of extra space, but of integrating sport into the paper and keeping editorial interest alive.

The separation is harmful in other ways. With the exception of a few highly-paid columnists, the salaries and fees paid to sports writers are often lower than those of comparable specialists (though, against that, the opportunities to travel are probably greater; while foreign news is increasingly gathered through a network of bureaus, men like Peter Wilson of the *Daily Mirror* and Desmond Hackett of the *Daily Express* have taken over from the Sefton Delmers and Frank Owens as the last of the great roving reporters). And it's harder for the staff man in sport to switch departments than it is for most.

Some sports editors like this arrangement, of course, preferring the calm of a backwater to the hidden currents of the mainstream. They make a mystery of managing the sports page, convincing the editorial board that it would be unwise to tamper. There was one sports editor whose removal was constantly plotted because, in design and general interest, his pages had not kept pace with the rest of the paper. Yet he survived every coup. His secret was that he had convinced the management that only he could cope with the logistics of bringing out the regional editions. The pages might not read very well, but at least they went to press on time.

The more ambitious sports editors work to break down the barrier, influence leaders, move sports features of wider appeal to inside pages and take a critical interest in the rest of the paper. But they meet opposition, not all of it open enough to be successfully countered. It may come in a negative way from proprietors who only respond with enthusiasm to their own rather special pursuits, such as racing or sailing. More destructively it may reflect that peculiarly English antagonism which intellectuals feel towards sport – perhaps an over-reaction to the absurd claims made for sport as a character builder or, as one sports editor suggested, to the type of school games captain who was insufferably good at everything. Certainly there are some editors who are totally uninterested in sport; William Rees-Mogg of *The Times* is one, and – though there may be other explanations – the sports page has not evolved under him as dramatically as other sections.

Obviously in life-and-death terms, sport is not 'important', and no sports writer would dispute it. During the Mexico City uprising at the time of the last Olympic Games, Brasher and McIlvanney acknowledged this by covering the demonstrations instead of the rehearsals in the stadium. John Rodda, the athletics correspondent of the *Guardian*, dictated a confused but vividly honest account of being caught in the militia gunfire. And at Brno last summer, David Saunders of the *Daily Telegraph* switched from the world cycle championships to the riots that marked the anniversary of the Czech invasion. But beyond accepting these priorities, it shouldn't have to be argued that activities which engage millions of people must be worth serious treatment by the press.

More specifically, newspapers are alarmed by the sheer volume of sports news which is produced every day of the year. They regard it as a monster which has to be controlled or it will eat up every inch of space. David Astor, editor of *The Observer*, once said to a former sports editor: 'If the world were going to end tomorrow, the sports page would still demand its quota of space for the 2.30 at Uttoxeter.' To which the sports editor replied, reasonably enough, that even if the world were going to end tomorrow, the 2.30 at Uttoxeter would still be run.

Newspapers might be more sympathetic to its demands if the sports page demonstrably paid its way. But it makes very little direct contribution to advertising revenue. On the Continent advertising space on the sports page is a premium position; in this country only football pool promoters, sports goods manufacturers, drink, tobacco and shaving accessory firms choose to appear there. Indirectly sport builds the circulation on which advertising rates depend. According to Fleet Street legend, the *Daily Worker*'s postwar boom was largely due to the success of its racing tipster. And whether this is true or not (the *Morning Star*, as it's now called, denies it), it's perfectly credible. But as long as Fleet Street works by hunches instead of market research, the exact financial return from the sports page will remain in doubt.

The attitude of the *Guardian* towards horse racing touches on several of these points. Some eighty years ago, the then *Manchester Guardian* did report racing; but during the 57-year editorial reign of C. P. Scott (1872–1929), this service was dropped out of a growing Liberal and nonconformist conviction that work people shouldn't be offered any encouragement to gamble. This view went unopposed until the early 1960s when the paper began to publish rather flabby colour pieces on the classics, treating them rather like quaint folk customs which the readers themselves might not have come across.

Developments were slow, for which the likeliest explanation (and the one accepted by members of the staff) seems to lie in the character of the editor, Alastair Hetherington, an urbane, intellectual Scot whose interests were about as remote as one could imagine from the pastimes of the English countryside. But

in 1967 the first decisive step was taken. Under the influence of
Peter Gibbings, who had recently come over from *The Observer* to
become the *Guardian*'s managing director, and with the support of
the sports department, it was agreed in principle that the paper
should carry regular racing reports and tips – though not the full
racing service which would give results and the next day's runners.
This became practice when Richard Baerlein, *The Observer*'s racing
correspondent, began writing for the *Guardian* in mid-week.

When this chapter was written last October, the internal debate
on whether or not to carry the full service seemed to be coming to
a head. But what had once been a critical moral question was now
simply one of economics. Baerlein's column had been a great
success; he was at that time the leading tipster. And while racing
was still only a half measure, the paper couldn't make the most
of his reputation. On the other hand the full service would run to
around £50,000 a year, including the cost of taking on specialist
sub-editors and printing extra pages thirty days a year. Racing
subs form their own little aristocracy on whose accuracy the fortunes of the punters depend.

Yet for that £50,000 – the equivalent of adding five foreign
correspondents to the staff – the paper couldn't be sure of putting
on a single extra reader. All it would do was remove the last
remaining excuse for a potential *Guardian* reader to take another
paper. By January 1970 this was accepted as a sufficient argument,
and a full racing service was introduced.

Beyond economic qualms like these, there can be broad and
justified misgivings about the basic journalistic quality of sports
pages. If their characteristic weakness in the serious papers has
been a rejection of general news values in favour of a remote, bird's
eye view from the top of the stand, they have had the opposite
failing in the popular papers – an overeagerness to build up trivia
into news. In the popular world there are no interesting matches,
only fantastic triumphs and fiascos. Motorcyclists and racing
drivers appropriately roar into victory; but so do sprinters, golfers
and cricketers (oh, the roar of the willow), and every goal is
blasted into the back of the net. John Arlott tells the story of one
provincial football reporter arriving late in the press box and
asking another, 'Which side started with a rush, Harold?' There's
always the temptation for the reporter to over-dramatize, for if
he keeps to the prosaic facts, he's likely to write himself off the
back page.

The pressure is to create heroes, and then turn on them when they do something less than heroic; athletes, febrile, sensitive creatures at the best of times, suffer particularly from this treatment. There is encouragement to pick up dressing-room gossip which goes far beyond a legitimate background interest. One rugby correspondent found he was getting nowhere by dutifully reporting the play; but he had instant success with a story about a player who kicked his goals in borrowed boots. That's the sort of stuff he sends in now; in conversation, though, he has the most accurate recall of complex passing movements of anyone in the press box. The talent is wasted.

As any provincial paper knows, one story about a local couple's broken marriage is worth ten about foreign disasters. But sports pages take this very naturally stronger interest in kith and kin to the point where they have a reputation of being among the most chauvinistic in the world. This scarcely needs illustration; but instances that come to mind are the slow recognition by the popular press of the existence of European soccer, and even now an almost total lack of interest in the fact that secretly, behind the iron curtain, Rumanian rugby has grown strong enough to challenge France. (Serious papers can be exonerated on the first count, almost entirely through Brian Glanville's writing in the *Sunday Times*, but not on the second.)

Even simple illiteracy exists on the back page. A recent sports column in the *Evening News* began: 'The eleven o'clock shadow on the face of British athletics . . . came home to roost at the White City yesterday evening.' Could that have passed under the sub's ball-point pen on any other page?

These faults remain because, in the present climate of press opinion, the writers lack confidence in sport as a vital, absorbing area of interest for its own sake, which hasn't any need for manufactured heroes and punchy writing.

As a footnote to the argument, there's a surprising lack of any British sports magazine to compare with the American *Sports Illustrated*, put out by the Time-Life group. It sets a pretty high standard of writing, and though, by repute, it took nine years to reach a break-even point it is now said to make more money than *Life*. In 1965 Clive Irving, then managing editor of IPC magazines, had the idea of filling this gap and asked me if I'd like to be editor.

The publication was to have been called *Now* – a title chosen less for what it said than for the fact that it didn't mention sport – and was to spread outside the conventional fields of sport. It was to be as much concerned with sailing, winter sports, holidays and that area (largely ignored by newspapers) which is expressed in the difference between camping (wet Scouts trying to light damp twigs with two matches) and *le camping* (the portable barbecue outside the blue canvas bungalow). Whether weekly, fortnightly or monthly, an unsettled question, *Now* was to be expensive and glossy enough to attract the best quality advertising.

We settled into Fleetway, an IPC subsidiary; Geoffrey Cannon, now editor of the *Radio Times*, designed a brochure which would have looked well on art directors' walls; and we commissioned material at colour magazine rates. Then things stopped happening. There was talk of forward advertising bookings being terrible that autumn. This was a hell of a time to bring out a new magazine. On one of the increasingly rare meetings with Irving, he wondered whether it wouldn't be better to bring out a daily sports paper like *L'Equipe*. What I gathered from rumours was that the company had lost faith in sport – however luxuriously portrayed, with not a hint of muddy boots – as the basis of a commercially successful publication.

One day there was a fire on the floor above, and someone from personnel came to see me. The editor of *Teddy Bear Weekly* had lost his office; would I mind very much if he borrowed mine? No broader hint was needed.

8

The harlot's prerogative

JOHN PALMER

'The power of the old press barons to destroy governments may have disappeared, but a choice sentence or two from a bilious City editor can still help to send them on their way.' This view by a retired financial editor of the influence of contemporary financial journalism is neither jaundiced nor overstated. But it makes it all the more surprising that so little study has been made of the growth and evolution of the City pages of the national press. I will argue that not only has financial journalism had an obvious impact on the newspaper industry, but also on the evolution of the financial crises which have overtaken the British economy in recent years.

The might of the City journalist's pen is, in part, a reflection of the permanent economic and financial crisis with which we have learned to live. After thirty years of barely interrupted stability the economies of a large part of the western world are now punctuated by crises of inflation, deflation, devaluation and all the other maladies of late capitalism. Inevitably people have looked to the financial commentator to unravel the complicated interplay of market and other forces which produce crises. Yet his assessment of the causes of crisis can itself contribute to the form which the crisis takes.

In many ways the communications media stand at the crucial intersection between the world of finance and the world of Government. The manner in which the actions and intentions of pressures of the advertisers. Some papers, like the *Sunday Times*, allow their motoring correspondents to carry a sting but on other newspapers several writers on cars give no more than sycophantic appreciation. The columnists presumably fear that if they write too harshly, the car firms will withdraw advertisements, and that they, the journalists, will find themselves scapegoats.

In fact it never seems to happen like that, though there was a quaint incident a few months back in the West country when a local garage proprietor withdrew his advertising from the *Bath and Wilts Evening Chronicle* because he did not take to the local man's comparison of the Mini and the Honda. The paper stuck by the writer, and British Leyland, makers of the Mini, appropriately went on record in support of the journalist's right to say what he liked.

Perhaps the classic exercise of the admen's muscles in this country took place in 1961 when members of the Society of West End Theatre Managers, stung by some capsule theatre reviews by one Mr Puff in *The Observer*'s Quick Theatre Guide, withdrew almost all advertisements. *The Observer*, weak at the time because of its editorial stand against the 1956 Suez invasion, fought for several weeks but in the end had to compromise by curbing Mr Puff's activities. (During the battle the *Sunday Times*, *The Observer*'s principal competitor, did not support its rival by also banning theatre advertisers from its columns.)

Papers with a tradition of radical journalism like *The Observer* and the *Guardian*, have often been flamboyantly and inspiringly reckless about the effect of their text on advertisers. But if these two papers are the bravest, the harsh reality is that only the handful which have invulnerable circulations are able to withstand to any degree the erosive effects of the advertisers.

One of the ironies of Fleet Street is that some of the papers which are journalistically the most degenerate – *The People*, the *News of the World* and, in a different way, the *Expresses* – react in the toughest and most correct way to improper advances from the advertiser. *The People*, for example, is ruthless in its exploitation of sex, and tasteless and vulgar as a newspaper. But compare its treatment of that well-worn trick of the advertising agencies, advertising copy laid out to look like newspaper copy, with that of more reputable papers. Occasionally, the reputable ones will allow an advertisement of this type to nestle alongside ordinary editorial without any indication that it is an advertisement, or with that fact acknowledged only in the tiniest print. Not so *The People*. Atop of the copy will be a firm label, Advertisement, surrounded by ample white space and bordered by a strong rule so that that fact cannot be obscured.

The reality of the situation is that it is only the papers which monopolize the readership in their particular market, like the *Daily Mirror* (nearly 5 million circulation against the *Sketch*'s less than a million), the *Daily Telegraph* (getting on towards a million and a half against *The Times*'s 437,000 and the *Guardian*'s 293,000) or the papers which have 5 million plus circulations like *The People*, the *News of the World* and the *Sunday Mirror*, which can treat their advertisers brusquely.

The advertising agencies have few pressures which they can exert on these successful papers because they know these papers are needed in almost any advertising campaign they are planning. Even if they try, the advertisement departments within these papers can make little headway. 'We take the view,' one *Daily Mirror* adman told me with a mixture of respect and despair, 'that a man up there [Lee Howard, the editor] has a bloody good formula for selling newspapers and we don't want to muck it up for him'.

But where papers are less secure, where they are involved in a comparatively competitive circulation war – even papers like the *Sunday Times* (nearly one and a half million against *The Observer*'s 879,000 and the *Sunday Telegraph*'s 753,000) – there is less power to withstand pressures. Where they are positively weak, like the *Sketch* (870,000) and the pre-Murdoch *Sun* (951,000), there is likely to be less will to fight the advertiser. I asked one advertising man 'When you want to tell a paper that it's got a low circulation and that it had better damn well do what you tell it or you'll go to the *Mirror*, how do you put it?' 'Just like that,' was his reply. 'Only stronger.'

It is characteristic that all of the crudities I have so far quoted have come from low circulation papers. If a paper is weak, it can reach the point where it hardly questions what it carries. The *Sketch*, for example, seemed quite proud of their 'slip edition' of 11 July 1969, the front page headline of which read, 'Silvikrin Hairspray Soars to Over 32%. Sizzling sales boost it to multiple's brand leader'. Alongside the headline, Jeannette Harding, Silvikrin's Sunshine Girl, was pictured in a bikini. The 'slip edition' is, of course, pure stunt, a false front and back page appended to the normal day's edition and sent on limited circulation to chemists throughout the country.

The *Telegraph* magazine in its early nervous days also did something which now it would be unlikely to do. A magnificently illustrated four-page article on South West Africa contained no acknowledgement that it was an advertisement, apart from a tiny insertion at the bottom of the first page which admitted, 'This article has been provided by the South African Information Service, Trafalgar Square, London, WC2, from whom further information can be obtained.'

Almost inevitably, weak circulation publications will accept pressures from the advertisers. But one of the intriguing features about the newspaper business is that the writers who work in it have never really challenged the incursions of the advertisers. They have been allowed to intrude into our papers, not exactly unnoticed, but in the absence of debate. Even the National Union of Journalists, which has paid much attention to the question of advertising features, has merely produced advice for journalists asked to write them rather than attempted to wipe out the whole concept.

This is surprising because the journalist is very much the man who is in the front line. The pressures on the working journalist may not be as severe here as they are in the United States. An extremely capable features editor on a now defunct New York morning paper was demoted a few years back simply because he refused to commission an advertising orientated feature series. But the pressures on the British journalist are evident. Should he accept free air tickets? Should he say what he wants to about cars? Should he write advertising features? Invariably newspaper editors pick on weak figures within their office, men judged less likely to be able to find a job elsewhere, to write their advertising features. But occasionally even star writers are persuaded to perform. Why should Vincent Mulchrone, for example, the *Daily Mail* veteran word-smith, let us so far into his private life as to reveal that the 'curvaceous thing' pictured above is his wife, 'the only female second row forward in the history of Rugby. Well, she never actually *played*'? Why? Because he is about to tell the story of how she slimmed her way to respectability, a tale which is naturally attended by nearby advertisements on slimming.

Journalists generally have never quite worked out the correct reflex to the admen's approaches. The traditional attitude of journalists themselves to the admen is of course part of journalistic folklore. The two groups traditionally live in a state of mutual ignorance which verges at times on contempt. On one provincial newspaper I worked on the advertisement manager had only to enter the room for the features editor to rise, stretch himself and wander out of the other door as if on some errand. In Fleet Street, until recently, there has been little social and not much more professional liaison between the two. The consequences of this have sometimes been bizarre – as for example on the day last summer when a powerful *Sun* front-page photograph of a Vietnamese child who had lost her legs lay above an ad for the Army, 'You'll Go Great Guns in the Army'.

But though it may gratify the journalist's spirit not to have to rub shoulders with the adman, his sense of independence is spurious. Even the tale of the *Sun*'s mix-up is cautionary. The army's advertising agency complained to the paper, and, according to a statement released shortly afterwards, was 'properly compensated'.

The debate about the value of advertising *per se* is an ancient one. Clearly there is a case in any society for advertising some items in newspapers, such as houses for sale, simply because that is a service to the reader. But in an ideal newspaper what other advertisements would be carried? Cigarettes? Whisky? Washing machines? The short answer is probably yes, but fewer of them.

In the society which we have contrived to build, however, such a debate is academic. The sad reality is that at the moment without advertisements, the British press could not survive. Indeed in the perilous state in which the British press now finds itself there is a case for arguing that the advertisement manager is marginally more important than the editor himself. The reasons for this are easily explained and little challenged in Fleet Street. National newspapers in this country cost roughly twice their selling price to produce. Popular papers depend marginally less on their advertisements than do quality ones, but none could survive without them.

The explanations for this situation, which does not occur anywhere else in the world and which does not apply to any other product in this country, are diverse. Partly it is that newsprint, the raw material upon which newspapers are printed, costs more in this country than anywhere else because of high import duties. Partly that the selling prices of newspapers in this country are low in comparison with selling prices abroad. Partly that production costs are ludicrously high, owing to widespread overmanning, high wages and a degree of fiddling. (A Saturday night driver of newspaper vans once boasted to me that he picked up £30 for one shift he worked on a reputable paper and then another £30 from another paper where a pal illegally signed him on.)

Thus it is that Fleet Street finds itself in the position of having only three daily morning papers which make a profit. The majority of daily papers (though not of Sundays) make a loss and exist only by courtesy of outside bodies, usually other papers in their group. *The Times* is being carried by the *Sunday Times* and the Thomson regional papers, the *Guardian* by the *Manchester Evening News*, the *Sunday Telegraph* by its sister paper the *Daily Telegraph*. The *Evening Standard* is supported by the *Daily* and *Sunday Expresses*. Until recently the *Sun* survived courtesy of *The People* and in the coming months will probably depend upon the *News of the World*. The *Daily Mail* and *Sketch* are generally thought to be carried by other Associated Newspapers' publications, including the massive circulation *Evening News*, but that particular group is so shy that it will not confirm or deny the fact.

The problem is how to avoid this. Most journalists would not warm to the idea of Government subsidies for newspapers. They would argue that if all papers were to receive subsidies then the Government's leverage on the press would be too strong: that if only the ailing ones were to receive money, the aid would be unfair to the more efficient papers and might prop up plainly bad papers. For the conceivable future, therefore, it seems as though newspapers are to remain dependent on their advertisers, and the debate which must begin should revolve around the terms on which they must live side by side.

One of the key factors in this, and one which is constantly overlooked, is the efficiency of the advertising departments of the newspapers themselves. One of the major reasons for the decline of newspapers in this country in recent years has been the incompetence of their advertising departments. Until recently, the average newspaper representative, the Gabardene swine, as the advertising agency men used to term them, tended to believe that his brylcreemed hair and jaunty manner were his main selling points. At the top of the advertising departments, if the opinions of the advertising agency men can be believed, the standard was if anything rather worse. Until two or three years ago there were few newspaper advertising executives who had any real grasp of marketing or were able to outline a detailed statistical case to advertising agencies. 'We on the agency side found ourselves talking two languages,' one senior man told me. 'The language we spoke amongst ourselves and the one we talked to the newspaper chaps.' No wonder then that with the advent of commercial television in the mid-1950s the papers found themselves in trouble. In the late 1950s, television's share of the advertisers' expenditure rose dramatically. In 1956, its first year, it was 3·4 per cent. Four years later it was 17·5 per cent. Today television takes more than half of the whole advertising revenue.

Until commercial television, newspapers had lived in a virtual monopoly situation for years. But from the start television began giving them a battering. They creamed off some of the best representatives. 'You had to feel sorry for the newspapers,' one agency man told me. 'Unlike television they were stuck with the problem of the faithful servants, with the incompetents, the lame, the crippled and the blind, who had worked for them for years.' These men never really found a solution for competing with television. 'It was an old saying on our side of the business,' says John Hughes, Hobson Bates's media director, 'that if you told one newspaper that another newspaper had won the account, you had a three-hour battle on your hands: but if you said it was going to a television company, they just picked up their bags and left.'

One of the tragedies of the communications industry in this country is that it has come to be expected that its development will follow the pattern of development in the United States, that in other words in the television age newspapers will go down like skittles for want of advertising. In reality, there is no reason for this to happen here. Newspapers in this country are potentially in a very powerful position *vis-à-vis* other media. Their central advantage over television is that the British press is national, coast to coast, and has a combined audience of 90 per cent of households. No American paper has any significant sales beyond its local circulation. Furthermore, newspapers in this country do not have such stiff competition from the magazine field. Magazines like *Life, Newsweek, Time* and *Esquire* garner many advertisements that newspapers in this country should acquire. In fact in this country, at the present time there is a shortage of media – unlike the United States – and although as the number of television channels increases, and as colour television spreads, the advantages of newspapers may slightly diminish, they will nevertheless remain a potentially very attractive medium for advertisers.

One of their attractive features to advertising men is their newsiness. There is a theory in the advertising field that it is easier to launch new items in a media which is also dealing with news than in one which is not. This, combined with the general fear of advertising men that the options open to them will be whittled down, is probably one of the main reasons why they themselves have been so active in the fight to assist the press to sharpen itself up. For years the advertising men have been pressing the newspapers to innovate in the advertising field. Committees of the Institute of Practitioners in Advertising have made recommendation after recommendation to the newspaper publishers. One of their successes has been to persuade the newspapers to accept colour advertisements within the main body of their papers. They have also pressed newspapers to regionalize adverts (a coming development), to give discounts for large advertisers and to give more flexible cancellation dates, a step recently taken by the *Guardian*'s comparatively newly appointed advertising chief, Gerry Taylor, who halved the cancellation period.

But the really crucial factor in persuading the newspaper business of its need to sharpen itself up came during the financial recession during the winter of 1966–7. It is no accident that several key posts within the advertising departments of newspapers have changed hands recently and that a new crop of executives, many of them with experience of television and some with knowledge of agency work itself, have come in. There were several firings and some retirements at normal retiring age. Taylor, who came in when his predecessor retired in the normal way, was formerly a media director with Ogilvy and Mather, one of the bigger advertising agencies. The man who inspired the 'Avant Guardian, Avant you seen it yet' ad, he is a complete advertising man, adept and forceful enough to be both a huge help and a danger to his paper. Taylor maintains very firmly that he likes the *Guardian*'s independent style as a newspaper, its integrity. That does not mean, however, that he does not think that there should be some changes in the shaping of the paper. 'The newspaper business,' he says, 'is the only business I know of where the advertiser has no say in the shaping of the product.' Taylor is too canny to state publicly whether he regrets that or not. I myself, were it true, would be only too happy about it. For one of my fears is that with the increasing efficiency of the marketing and advertising men will come unhappy changes in the newspapers.

The advertising men have, of course, been a shaping force behind the scenes for a long time now. Few outsiders, and not enough journalists themselves, realize that even so fundamental a point as the size of the paper is often dependent on the number of ads to be found in that issue. Most newspapers decide the number of pages in a particular day's edition by counting the number of ads they have received for that edition. Likewise, the shape of the papers has often been in some way moulded to the need for getting advertisements. Sport, for example, seems to be losing its place on the back page because it is not a good advertising magnet.

But recently, with the tense situation surrounding the publishing of newspapers becoming more and more marked, the admen have been getting more influential. Nowhere has this happened more obviously than in the Thomson press.

When Roy, later Lord, Thomson swept into this country conquering all with a captivating blend of Canadian charm and dollars, a quiet revolution began within newspaper advertising departments. One of the first steps Thomson took was to beckon out of retirement the doyen of American advertising men, an old chum, George Pappas, who duly travelled to this country to transform the classified advertising scene. Before long, well-drilled teams of classified advertising sales girls emerged in all Thomson's major provincial papers and at the *Sunday Times*. The classified ads department was given a new status within the office. The girls were trained in pressure selling techniques and they pushed up sales enormously. Thus Thomson, with the benefit of years of observation of his newspapers on the North American continent, was the first proprietor of British newspapers really to see the potential for classified advertising, a honeypot which must almost by definition elude television. It says a great deal for Thomson's foresight that classified advertising has recently increased dramatically in national newspapers and is now being spoken of as a potential saviour of several papers, not least the *Guardian*.

Thomson's approach to classified ads is typical. For the Thomson press must be praised for being the first group to tackle the central issue facing newspapers at present, the issue of how to come to terms with the advertising men. Their solution has been to restyle their papers so that they get more readers, and above all, more advertisements. Thomson's organization has given the kiss of life to several newspapers, and the only question which anybody can reasonably ask is whether a better kiss could have been effected and whether the papers which have been revived could have re-emerged in a more healthy state.

The Thomson Organization has done much for several of its provincial papers (or regional papers, as it likes to call them) such as *The Scotsman* and the *Western Mail*, injecting money, investing wisely,

ploughing profits back. But the import of the Thomson revolution
– and it is a revolution because its characteristics are now being
aped by other companies – is best seen by examining Thomson's
two best-known papers, *The Times* and the *Sunday Times*.

Even taking into account the expansion in serious readership
in Britain, the circulation success of both these papers has been
phenomenal. When Thomson took over the *Sunday Times* in
August 1959, its circulation was 884,265. Ten years later it was
1,492,689. In a much shorter period of ownership he has almost
doubled the circulation of *The Times*: when he bought it late in
1966 its circulation was 290,000; now it is 437,000. Advertising
revenue for both papers has increased accordingly.

Between the two papers, however, there is one obvious difference. *The Times*, however much ground it has made up, could still
find itself in difficulties principally because it has not yet become
competitive with the *Daily Telegraph*. The *Sunday Times*, on the
other hand, easily leads its field despite revivals by both *The
Observer* and the *Sunday Telegraph*. Since the two papers are in
such different states of health, their virtues and faults are likely
to be distributed in different proportions.

Where it seems to me that Thomson has done a disservice to
the British press is that he has developed what I can only call,
for want of a better word, the consensus newspaper. What he has
done, to put it in the most ungenerous way I can, is to make not
one or two pages into crude advertising vehicles, but to make
whole newspapers, 40, 50, even 90 pages of them, into sophisticated advertising vehicles.

It started, I suppose, with the colour section. Thomson is
generally agreed to have been brave to pioneer the colour sections,
but that does not disguise the fact that basically these are
advertising vehicles and that their introduction into the quality
field, into the *Sunday Times* and *The Observer* particularly, has
altered the character of those papers.

The *Sunday Times* colour section takes anything up to 60 per
cent of its pages as advertising. In the words of its own advertisements, 'Every Sunday, the *Sunday Times* magazine presents a
showcase of the world's finest photo-reportage. And, of course, it
is also a showcase for the advertiser – four million readers who
comprise a profitable market for every kind of product.'

Even that part of the paper which is not advertisements would
seem foreign to the discriminating reader of a decade ago. The
colour section's inclination towards the trendy and the ephemeral

is generally acknowledged. Some articles, like Richard West's series on Africa, are good journalism by any standards, but by and large the subjects chosen are not challenging. Were it not for their jumpy treatment, they would not seem out of place in the old *Tatler*.

But though the magazine is advertisement-orientated, its attitude in detail towards advertisers is impeccable. This is very illustrative of the Thomson technique. Godfrey Smith, the colour section's editor, describes advertisers as being paying guests in his hotel and having to observe the house rules: and it is true that one rarely sees in his magazine the crude linking of text and advertisements examined earlier. Car criticisms are often pungent, feature articles can be satirical, even at the expense of advertisers. One cannot help feeling, however, that these are the little luxuries of a magazine basically beamed at the advertiser, and so successful on its own terms that it can afford to be a little churlish at times.

But if it started with the colour section, consensus journalism has not been content to stay there. The genie was out of the bottle. You feel that by hook or by crook the *Sunday Times* now intends to net every reader in the country who earns more than £2,000 a year, whatever his intelligence, his intellect or his tastes: and that furthermore it intends to capture every advertisement aimed at that market. The result is that even a paper with as many virtues as the *Sunday Times* (and 'Insight' did pioneer a penetrating investigatory technique) is beginning to appear schizophrenic. Who would have thought a few years back that a quality paper would carry something so consumer-orientated as the 'Look' section in the transformed arts portion of the paper? Reading the *Sunday Times* every week, you can almost feel the Thomson minds ticking. How will we halt the *Sunday Telegraph*'s unexpected circulation rise? Revive the court circular, take sport off the back page. What about the readership in the Principality? Let's turn out an investiture leading article in Welsh. Are we missing out on the ambitious provincial socialite? A large wedge of Alan Brien's name-dropping on the back. And then, of course, there's always Lord Snowdon.

But the interesting point, and a characteristic one of the Thomson press, is that though the paper has tended to be shaped to please the advertisers, and though the style of writer encouraged on the paper has changed, the paper does not directly, crudely, fawn on the advertiser in its writing. It very firmly draws its line. Thus, although the business section is a perfect

vehicle for advertisements, and gains a great number, its writers
never link copy with ads. Indeed, sometimes you feel that the
writers are itching to have a go at the advertisers. Stephen Aris's
story last summer revealing that Metal Box, the company which
makes steel cans, was irritated by British Steel's 'Can Can'
advertising campaign, hardly deserved its prominent place on
page one of the business news. Were it not for the fact that the
colour section had large 'Can Can' advertisements, I suspect that
it might never have been used.

Likewise, the *Sunday Times* gives ample space to motoring and
reaps an immense amount of motoring advertisements, particularly from the manufacturers of prestige cars. The *Sunday Times*
has two permanent motoring correspondents plus a number of
writers – Stirling Moss for example – who guest for them. But the
standard of criticism is high: Maxwell Boyd's criticisms are as
vigorous as any in the British press. Moreover, the *Sunday Times*,
particularly in the days when Michael Cudlipp (now with *The
Times*) was in charge of late production, went to great pains to
ensure that a motoring column should never be aligned with an
ad dealing with the same model, even if this meant tearing out an
advertisement at the last minute.

With *The Times*, the calculations which the paper's management
makes are more obvious. *The Times* again is a paper which does as
much as it can to ensure that crudities of linking ads and copy do
not occur. A neat illustration of their sophistication and integrity
on this level is to compare the editions of the *Daily Mail* and
The Times on Saturday, 6 September. Both papers that day had
holiday articles concerning winter holidays. The *Mail*, which
began with the bland observation that 'many tour operators are
offering really low-priced holidays this coming winter', concluded
by praising two of their principal surrounding advertisers –
Swedish Lloyd and Normandy Ferries. These two companies also
advertised in *The Times*'s winter holiday page, but they were not
mentioned in the attendant editorial copy. Instead John Carter,
The Times's travel correspondent, wrote a sharp and thoughtful
piece about the dangers surrounding package holidays and
shunned the temptation to mention any particular firm.

But *The Times*'s willingness to let its writers have their head
should not deceive. *The Times* is desperately concerned with
reaping ads and does make compromises. Indeed it is within *The
Times* building that the advertising men and the marketing men
have become most impudent. The advertising men make a point

of making personal contact with editorial and frequently suggest that articles featuring various merchandise should be written. As for the marketing men, some idea of their ambitions can be gained from an internal report which they produced recently, recommending, without any apologies or graceful bows to editorial, that the 'policy of the women's feature should be to develop a market place for advertisers'. The report goes on to regret that 'at present women's features attempt to cover all women's interests' and to recommend that editorial should be concentrated on more commercial subjects and that women should be catered for in these pages as 'housewives and consumers'.

As the Thomson men moved into *The Times*, some crucial changes followed. Shortly after the takeover, for example, a commercial property column was inaugurated, which, though vigorously written in *Times* style, has proved an excellent advertising magnet. Likewise, the men's fashion column, which has harvested hundreds of ads, has become more frequent. More than on the *Sunday Times* the principle seems to apply in Printing House Square that if a section is not valuable as an advertising vehicle, it is not valuable at all. The history of *The Times* Saturday Review points a lesson. Launched with a great deal of excitement, the Review in general and the books section in particular, failed to attract the hoped-for amount of advertising. So, according to Thomson logic, the review became a problem child. Instead of realizing that the problem with the books section was simply the quality of the reviews, they panicked. One minute they banished the Review: the next it regained its separate identity. All last summer the argument continued within Printing House Square about what to do with the poor Saturday Review. The problem is still not resolved.

The story is much the same wherever you look in today's *Times*. The paper has one of the best organized advertising departments in Fleet Street. Its advertising team is three times the size of the *Guardian*'s. Every man on the display side of the department is a specialist in his field. The classified section has been overhauled dramatically since the Thomson takeover. But the efficiency of these departments is cutting both ways. They are serving editorial well, but they are also influencing editorial. No better index of the increased advertising consciousness of *The Times* can be found than the increased number of commercially-orientated special pull-out supplements. No better insight into what they mean to the reader can be found than looking on the tube each morning and counting how many of these fat supplements are left behind untouched.

Apologists for the Thomson press would argue that the rejected pull-out supplements do not matter. They would say that in *The Times* and the *Sunday Times* there is something which appeals to everyone. They would claim that both those papers have been livened up since Thomson took over. They would point to the circulation figures as proof and they would defend any noticeable straining after advertisements as only common sense. To a degree they are right. But the feeling remains that it could all have been done in so much more graceful a way. In essence what the Thomson press has tried to do is to appeal to a wider audience, to slice off a larger cross-section of our population than has ever been done before. They have gone about this not by producing characterful papers but by religiously catering for tastes, not by persuading the reader that there is something he desperately wants to read but by making him feel that each edition will contain something which he cannot afford to miss. But there is a well-documented danger in trying to please too many people, and that is that you end up by satisfying none.

6

The woman complex

SUSANNE PUDDEFOOT

Gentleman, I am a very young woman, born of parents of
some little Quality . . .; it was my Calamity about two years
since (for since Black and White cannot blush, I venture
under this Skreen to make you my Confessors) to be so
seduced, as to give up the very Soul of Beauty, my Honour,
to an infamous Rifler, with whom I secretly continued this
vile and unhappy Conversation, for near a Twelvemonth
together. After this, a person of very great Honour and
Worth, trebly my Superior in Birth, in Fortunes infinitely,
fell honourably in Love with me, and after two months
courtship, possessed me . . . the more I dote on him and he
the like on me, a rueful remembrance makes me consider
myself so much the more unworthy of him; a hundred daily
and hourly Horrours haunt me, telling my conscious Soul
what Delusion and Pollution I brought to his Bed . . . In
this Love-Sick and Shame-sick Condition, pray give a dis-
tressed Lady some Advice, (for from those that know me I
must not ask it) how to support her self in this deplorable
Calamity . . .

   Answer Well, Mournful fair unknown . . . if all the private
wounds of Feminine Honour felt your Remorse and Pain,
I'm afraid we should have but a sickly Age and a drooping
World. However, to consider your Request and act our part
of a healing Councellor, We'll state your whole Case . . . Did
you make your self Happy in the honourable Embraces of

F

the best of Husbands in a little Hypocrisie? Jacob obtained
the highest of Blessings, transferr'd even to Posterity, by a
false Neck and false Hands, the most notorious of Cheats,
and the boldest of lyes. You brought Guilt to his bed, tis
true, but a truly and nobly repented Guilt. Infamy (the
more substantial and sensible wrong) you brought none, for
your sin lyes concealed from the world. Your husband, for
his part, tasted no fainter nor weaker sweets in your
Embraces for having a Rose-bud crop'd before him: For
Ignorance keeps up Devotion . . .

In 1693, with this anonymous reader's letter and its reply, *The
Ladies' Mercury* made its brief but entertaining debut. It is the
first known publication for women. The publisher, a bookseller
named John Dunton, had already started a twice-weekly informa-
tion-and-gossip sheet called *The Athenian Mercury*; his editorial
in *The Ladies' Mercury* promised that its 'narrow speculation'
would not trespass upon the 'Athenian Province' of 'Examination
of Learning, Nature, Arts, Sciences and indeed the whole world'.
This would not be necessary since it was to be devoted to 'that
little sublunary, Woman' and, it went on, 'Whilst Religion and
Heaven, and other sublimer Points are your Gamaliel studies, we
are for sitting down with Martha's humbler part . . .'
The humbler part is, of course, 'a little homely cookery, the
dishing-up of a small Treat of Love, etc.' Jocular or not, the
definition is archetypal. The editorial preoccupations and moral
assumptions of modern women's journalism are remarkably
similar; only the tone has changed, to one of serious, almost
religious conviction.
During the following 150 years, a polarity steadily developed in
publishing between the masculine, newspaper world of business,
politics and public life and the feminine, magazine world of dress,
gossip and social behaviour – the one dominated by events and
the other by sentiments. By the early Victorian period woman had
become, as Steele had gloomily prophesied, a bloodless ideal of
refinement – 'a being', according to one magazine editorial, 'of
delicate perceptions, tremblingly alive to the least infringement
of decorum; ever studying to please by unostentatious behaviour
and heartfelt benevolence, anxious to make all around her easy
and happy, polite without ceremony, modest without bashful-
ness, commanding all sorts of attention by her retiring and un-
asking lowliness, and with a humble heartfelt piety'.

But by the turn of the mid-century two new currents of feeling begin to make themselves felt in women's magazine journalism. The first goes back to Mary Wollstonecraft in 1792 – the women's rights movement. Picked up and given political validity and wider public discussion in the 1860s by John Stuart Mill it immediately found published expression in magazines like *The Englishwoman's Review* (1866) and *Woman's World*, later the *Kettledrum* (1866), and, later still, *Woman*, edited by Arnold Bennett (1890) and *The Women's Dreadnought*, edited by Sylvia Pankhurst (1913).

The second current is exemplified by the *Englishwoman's Domestic Magazine*. Sam Beeton, who began it in 1852, anticipated the needs of the new kind of emergent middle-class woman, the small tradesman's or professional man's wife, who wanted advice on what previous centuries had assumed women would know from instinct or their mother's example: how to run a home. Sam's wife, Isabella, undertook to tell her, and the tremendous response to the *Englishwoman's Domestic Magazine* resulted in the book which has become this country's byword for the art of cookery and domestic economy.

In spite of Isabella's early death in 1865, the magazine continued to run in various forms until 1881. It is from this period that the significant words 'home' and 'household' begin to appear, with increasing frequency, in the titles of the increasing numbers of magazines for women. The most successful of these, Northcliffe's *Home Chat*, ran for over sixty years, until 1959. And, in spite of his spectacularly unsuccessful experiment in 1903 of a newspaper for women (later to become the *Daily Mirror*), Northcliffe's provision of a 'Woman's Realm' feature in the new *Daily Mail* of 1896 signalled the beginning of newspapers' attempts to cash in on the growing readership and advertising potential among women.

And it is from this period that a certain stereotyped image of woman begins to solidify in the women's press: a combination of artificial hothouse Lady; militant, banner-waving Virago; and dedicated managing Housewife, up to her elbows in flour and a child's primer in her hands. This triple image still survives, only slightly modified, as the remote, doe-eyed Model; the independent anti-feminine Careerwoman; and the eternal Housewife, still dedicated, still managerial, still up to her elbows in flour, but now running her local playgroup or typing up the minutes of the P.T.A. For the most part, the twentieth-century women's press, today embodying a hundred or so titles, as well as regular features or pages for women in all the major national and provincial newspapers, has continued to pursue the propagation of these stereotypes.

The increased sophistication of printing techniques, and the growth in circulation figures which took place after both world wars, has led to a greater degree of choice – from the glossy *Vogue* to the humble *Red Star Weekly*, from the serious and wide-ranging women's pages in the *Guardian* or *The Times* to the frothy entertainment provided for them in the *Daily Sketch* or the *Daily Mail*'s 'Femail'. And whether the publication is a mass circulation weekly or a quality newspaper, dress and domestic matters remain the most important topics. The late 1950s and '60s have been a period of new developments in the women's press. The year 1955 saw the publication of *She*, a racy, down-the-market but very wide general interest magazine; 1955 the Mirror Group's second attempt at a women's newspaper – the *Woman's Sunday Mirror*; 1959 the restyling of the frail old society magazine *Queen* into a trend-setting glossy. In the late 1950s, too, a host of teenage magazines sprang up, ranging from the fashion-conscious *Honey* to strip-romance magazines like *Mirabelle*, *Valentine* and *Romeo*.

In the early 1960s the quality newspapers also expanded the women's coverage with the Sundays (especially *The Observer* and *Sunday Times*) running large, entertaining and often quite tough feature pages for women. In this field the *Daily Telegraph* had had a head start of some ten years over the rest of the quality newspapers – due to the foresight of Evelyn Garrett. Appointed women's editor in 1940, when most women's features had been drastically curtailed, she pioneered, according to her obituary, 'a new style of topical and informative page for women readers that was far removed from the limited round of social gossip, fashion and recipes of women's pages in pre-war years'. That the *Telegraph*'s women's page was responsible at least in part for its high circulation figures is shown by the fact that at one point in the early 1960s women represented over half of its total readership. Of late, however, its comfortable position seems to have rendered it somewhat staid in tone.

In 1965 a 'new magazine for the new kind of woman' appeared in the form of the glossy *Nova* and in May of the following year Sir William Haley hired a complete new team of women to re-design and expand *The Times* women's page both in size and range of content, on a daily instead of weekly basis. A few weeks later *The Observer* also expanded and redesigned its women's section, and the *Guardian*, which had already expanded its women's features on the advice of research consultant Mark Abrams, followed suit again with a redesigned full page feature entitled 'Women's Guardian' in 1969.

However, the most recent development has been for the women's pages of *The Observer* to change their title from 'Hers' to 'Ego' and for the *Sunday Times* women's features to be restyled on similar lines, with the title of 'Look'. Both are supposed to appeal to both sexes: what this betokens for the future of women in newspapers is hard to say.

By contrast the most interesting new magazine departure is represented by two monthly home magazines started by the Thomson organization in 1967: the new factor is the form of distribution – through supermarkets only. The *Daily Mail*'s pull-out tabloid 'Femail' is an interesting departure; the popular papers have for a long time past incorporated their women's features into the rest of the feature coverage. There are arguments both for and against this editorial apartheid: certainly in those quality papers where the women's page editor has been given some degree of autonomy, the discussion of social problems such as divorce, illegitimacy, disablement, housing, poverty and so on has often been considerably more courageous than elsewhere in the parent paper. But so far this adventurous spirit has barely touched the women's magazines.

In terms of content and approach, the current field of popular women's magazines, although increasingly carefully structured by modern marketing techniques to appeal to different age and income groups, is a largely homogeneous one. So much so that a recent advertising campaign was driven to say: 'If you think all women's magazines are the same, take a look at *Woman's Own*.'

This is to some extent due to the fact that the top-selling weeklies (*Woman, Woman's Own, Woman's Realm* and *Woman's Weekly*), as well as the major monthly and teenage magazines, are all owned by the International Printing Corporation.

The magazine division of IPC had in 1967–8 a total sales revenue of £48,036,000; of this, advertising sales brought in £20,150,000, and circulation sales £22,011,000; in the case of the weeklies mentioned above and the monthlies, income from advertising exceeded income from sales by over 40 per cent. With the deduction of the very high printing, promotion and other costs, pre-tax profits amounted to £3,818,000 of which the four weeklies, with a total circulation of around 8 million and a readership of perhaps three times that number, provided 63·9 per cent of the total. Popular women's magazines are therefore a lucrative and powerful medium, the success and appeal of which are founded on the refinement of a formula which has evolved over nearly 250 years. The staple content of this formula is, primarily, a heavy domestic preoccupation, with strong emphasis on the deployment of homemaking skills, backed by recipe leaflets as well as featured merchandise and shopping guidance.

The second staple of content is advice and exchange of views on emotional, social and family matters. The letters are, according to editors, their most popular feature: *Woman* actually has five – two problem features, two others advising on money and etiquette and such things as social service benefits, and 'Woman to Woman', a page of readers' anecdotes. Fashion and beauty is the third priority, with most of the magazines regularly offering cut-price garments, cosmetics or jewellery, as well as supplementary booklets on knitting, dressmaking, make-up, etc.

Advertising revenue closely follows this specialization: in food and soft drinks, the revenue of the women's magazine press for 1968 totalled over £5½ million, more than 50 per cent of the total spent in advertising as a whole; in cosmetics and toiletries, their advertising income of over £6 million represented 70 per cent of the total spent in the press. The total annual advertising expenditure in women's magazines was nearly £26 million.

This then is John Dunton's original recipe – 'a little homely cookery, the dishing up of a small treat of Love' – with the ingredients adapted and the method modernized to formulate a rich, mass-production cake.

To quote a popular modern definition, their aim is to 'teach women how to make woollies, jellies and love'. But now it has been elevated almost to the level of a philosophy, pursued with apparent conviction by writers and readers alike.

Apparently the closer the identification with the housewife role and the clearer the definition of the educational and socio-economic level of the readership, the greater the success of the publication. Outside the 'service sections' described, general interest features usually represent less than 10 per cent of editorial content. And even this may not be necessary. A striking example of this is provided by the two new Thomson organization home magazines, *Living* and *Family Circle*. Apart from their form of distribution – through supermarkets – they are unique in two other ways: they carry no fiction and none of what passes for general interest features – interviews with entertainment stars, cosy revelations about the royal family – in most other women's magazines. Their features are closely home-orientated, covering moving house, loneliness in the suburbs, how a parent-teacher association works.

In two years *Family Circle* and *Living* have reached respectively the highest and third highest circulation figures of all women's monthly magazines; so the policy seems to pay off. And according to the McKinsey report on IPC, they have the newly reconstituted Magazine Department fairly worried. The success of specialization is also demonstrated by the glossy *House and Garden* or the more down-the-market *Woman and Home*. It perhaps also accounts for the recent circulation gains of *Woman's Weekly*, the only one of the 'big four' weeklies not to have lost readers recently, and the one which is also more clearly aimed at its older and less well-off age group. It is also in this type of magazine that the least sense of editorial strain or ambiguity is felt.

In a way too, this applies even to the obverse of the housewife-identification syndrome, to be found at its extreme in the D. C. Thomson company's strip-cartoon romance magazines: in these the total aura of fantasy is only minimally impinged on by the painful realities of adolescent acne, broken romances or the need to earn a living.

Of the more down-to-earth teenage magazines, IPC's *Honey* and *19*, although pitched at a rather frenetic level of swinging gaiety, also gain their integral homogeneity from a fairly clearly defined market – the single working girl.

In my view, the more wide-ranging and 'emancipated' a magazine or its features, the greater is the sense of unease which their attempt to reconcile conflicting functions induces in the reader. Compared to the total role-identification of a *Mother and Baby* or the total fantasy of a *Romeo*, I find the butch, elbow-nudging raciness of *She* offensive, and decorous good sense of *The Lady* prissy, the sex-charged sensationalism of 'Femail' like a strip show, the ambidextrous conformity of the 'Look' and 'Ego' pages like an endless drag review and the anxiety-charged glamour of *Nova* like a drug-induced dream.

It is perhaps in *Nova*, also reputed to be causing its publishers some concern, that the strain currently shows most. With a pessimistically liberal outlook and a certain forensic relish, *Nova* has

made forays into subject-matter previously taboo in English
women's magazines – sexuality, politics, social problems – and
carried its hard-edged approach through even to its treatment of
fashion and beauty.

The by-products, it would seem, of this editorial approach have
been an unusually high male readership and a gradual falling-off,
after initial interest, of circulation growth. The recently appointed
new editor, committed to a policy of 'making the magazine more
feminine' yet feeling at the same time a desire to retain and
improve its treatment-in-depth approach to topics of public
debate, admits that this is like 'walking a tightrope'.

On the evidence of other attempts, bringing women's magazines
into wider contact with life outside the home is a risky under-
taking. The ill-fated *Woman's Mirror* was one example, eerily
evoking its predecessor of similar name sixty years earlier. It
started as a pop tabloid women's newspaper, was reformulated as
a gravure magazine in 1958 and survived comfortably enough
until 1962.

It was then face-lifted twice. The second time was in 1966:
it was given a new editor, a woman from the newspaper world
with a tough sense of topical actuality, who introduced much
stronger features, promoted with a heavy press and TV advertising campaign – and in only a matter of months had dropped a
huge amount of circulation and been absorbed in *Woman*. What
went wrong? The verdict of those involved was that 'we tried to
go too fast too soon' – in other words, that readers could not
accept a magazine that was outspoken, dealt with general topics,
etc. The point was, however, that these *particular* women – who
were in fact neither very young nor in the very well-off or well-
educated classes – could not take it.

Yet this experience has been fairly widely interpreted as
indicating that women in general cannot stand too much of a
certain kind of reality. One of IPC's senior editorial people, with
many years' experience of the women's magazine field, says quite
categorically: 'When we take them into the cerebral realms, they
do not buy.' The implications of this statement are wide. A
publication must have readers merely to exist, let alone to make
money. If it gives its readers what they want – and all the evidence
suggests that domestically-orientated magazines *are* what the
readers want – then it seems irrational to castigate the publishers
for providing it.

The argument that cultural conditioning determines readers'

expectations and capacities is, however, also valid. And in the case of women's magazines, the fact that they were originally intended as trivial amusements for the empty lives of first a leisured minority and subsequently the drab majority, has to a large extent left its mark on them. The grafting on to such a frail *raison d'être* of the compensatory 'service' element – the domestic information and advice – has resulted in a yet further level of ambiguity which is noticeable even in those, such as *Woman* or *Woman's Own*, where the service side is the overt selling platform.

The more important question is, then, not what they do but how they do it. In spite of the frequent editorial insistence on the informative service function of these magazines, the conflicting claim is almost as frequently made by their editors that they are intended as entertainment. In walking this particular tightrope, the effect they achieve seems to be one of persistent suspension over a deep chasm of unreality. This impression of being in an almost totally unreal world is one of the most striking impressions of reading women's publications, even though the component parts of the fabricated dream may well be real enough to all appearances. The effect is achieved in a number of fairly subtle ways.

The factor most frequently cited by critics is the visual confusion of advertising and editorial content – in my view something of a red herring. Advertisers can rarely eschew an insistent selling slogan or an equally insistent logotyped brand-name: this, to the practised reader, immediately proclaims 'advertisement'. Of course, not all readers are practised and some of them, as I have found, find it hard to believe that the appearance and content of advertisements are not under the control of the editors.

A more real and insidious danger of advertising, I think, is that by demanding 'related editorial' next to or near advertisements (i.e. a home decorating feature facing a furniture advertisement), or by only placing advertisements where the cross-section of readers most resembles their own potential market, advertisers can indirectly influence a publication's contents. Although this is a risk by no means confined to the women's press, it is more exposed to it and less able or inclined to reject it than most.

More serious, in my view, is the distortion of reality consistently practised in editorial content. This distortion can be achieved in two ways. The first is by a deliberate mingling of the elements of fantasy and reality. The fashionable model on whom clothes are photographed, a person totally unreal in relation to the reader's dimensions, is a cliché now – unthinkingly accepted and allowed for. But it has been known for a beauty 'make-over' story, even though based on a real person, to be photographed on a model. Even real-life stories are ghosted and reconstructed to resemble fiction (a technique not unknown elsewhere); indeed most of the writing aimed at women is written in a heightened personalized style that is essentially fictional. Much of the fiction for that matter is in first-person narrative; so too are letters and the popular columns of name writers. In more than one magazine, even the name and the comments of the sympathetic 'Aunt Aggie', who is in reality a panel of several experts, are fictional. On such is based the 'woman to woman' personal communication of which these magazines boast.

The second form of distortion is the use of dissociation. This, the common psychological process whereby a mental area of difficulty or conflict is split off into separate components, is common to many forms of communication: it is part of the myth-making machinery of the media. In the women's press it can be observed operating in a general way throughout, in the division of the concept 'woman' from person into different functions – wife, mother, cook, decorator, etc. – and is perhaps the origin of Marshall McLuhan's observation: 'Women have found that they have been robbed of their distinctive roles and turned into fragmented citizens in a man's world.' But dissociation operates more specifically in the sex-romance-love-marriage area, where the fiction provides the 'good' fantasy-romance-happiness element of the dichotomy and the problem letters the 'bad' factual-sex-unhappiness side; if fiction in women's magazines has any function other than residual or catchpenny, this is it.

One women's magazine editor has said that modern women's magazine fiction 'has to have a purpose, has to reflect life *as it's lived today*' (my italics). At the same time this editor's policy is that anything 'sensual, erotic or vulgar' is taboo in the publication.

Thus in women's magazines we are presented with two conflicting pictures. In the fictional one, according to a survey quoted by the BBC programme 'The Persuaders', 68 out of 70 stories had happy endings. Raymond Williams, in his Penguin *Communications*, analyses 72 women's magazine stories and remarks that he too thinks they are 'written to promote a particular psychological process in the reader'. He divides the stories into two main types: one in which the heroine adjusts to the situation (usually one of emotional difficulty) and the other in which 'the world adjusts to

the one is interpreted to the other affects the behaviour of both parties. It is no overstatement to describe City editors and economic commentators today as a guru caste. During times of great uncertainty and confusion the financial commentators alone appear to have the establishment's ear. When the nostrums of the old economic system are being widely distrusted the high priests of the City pages appear to offer doctrinal certainty in providing solutions to our economic problems. For many of our City editors (particularly those in the popular press, who have the greatest influence on the financial markets) solutions are always simple and straightforward. If they are not carried out it can only be because of the obstinacy, incompetence or villainy of the Government.

Yet how realistic is it to accept the impartial credentials of City editors? The great majority of leading City journalists are right wing. They work for right wing papers. They live and work in the overpoweringly right wing environment of the City.

Britain's economic crisis is not caused by City editors. The crisis lies in the very roots of Britain's economic history. But Britain's financial fortunes are not merely tied up with the country's basic economic condition. Sterling is an international currency. Its fortunes directly affect the ability of the British Government to tackle the economic problems. Yet the behaviour of sterling in the world money markets is often determined less by the facts of the country's economic situation than by the interpretation of those facts in the press. Interpretation and prognostication in the City press are as likely to affect the willingness of bankers and traders here and abroad to hold sterling as any set of economic statistics.

It is difficult, if not impossible, to distinguish between economic 'facts' and their manner of presentation. A simple example will show what I mean. As a result of successive balance of payments deficits the British Government has borrowed money from the international bankers. The popular financial press describes this situation as 'Britain's indebtedness'. No mention is made of the fact that while Britain owes more money to the bankers than we have in our official money and gold reserves, the value of the assets *owned by all British citizens abroad* far exceeds all the liabilities owed by British citizens and the state. Depending on what categories one uses Britain can be presented as a bankrupt debtor nation or a creditor nation. The choice of categories I believe to be determined by political or ideological considerations.

A number of influential economic and City commentators have presented the details of Britain's economic problems in terms and in a manner designed to arouse the maximum misgivings and apprehension in the minds of dealers in sterling and the financial markets at large. But the responsibility of the City press does not end there. There has been an alarming tendency in the past three or four years for City editors to give credence to rumours and talk of rumours in the financial markets on the flimsiest of evidence.

During one of the mini-runs on sterling during 1968, the scare was attributed to fears of a political crisis in the Government. This apparantly stemmed from 'reliable reports' received in the market about the imminent resignation of the Prime Minister; a resignation forced on him by his fellow ministers. Certain popular papers widely reported both the facts of the run and the underlying rumours on their City pages. The following day the run accelerated since dealers assumed that the fact that the rumours had been reported gave them authority. In the end it was discovered that the origin of the rumours lay in innocent but ill-informed lunch-time speculation in a City pub. Right wing papers are anxious to portray the Labour Government as lacking the ability to govern. To prove their thesis their City editors are all too often incapable of resisting the temptation to exploit financial uncertainties.

It is not only for the manner in which economic and financial news is presented that a large section of the City press may be criticized. After all the Government itself would seem to accept the approach to our problems shown by most City editors. Mr Wilson's Government can fairly claim to have proven itself to be as orthodox in financial matters as any post-war Conservative Government. Between the bankers and the British Government there at least appears to be a shared wisdom about policy priorities in times of crisis. But how is this wisdom actually communicated? How is it that just when the bankers are allegedly worrying about the amount we spend on, say, prescription charges, the Government comes to the conclusion that something must be done about it?

By suggesting what the bankers – or those holding sterling – expect of the Government during a crisis the financial press clearly place the Government on trial. If the City page headlines scream that without such and such a measure there will be a massive loss of confidence in sterling they precisely help to ensure such a loss of confidence if the policy is not forthcoming. There is no evidence that the financial world has been as united in its policy recommendations to the British Government as the financial press would have us believe. It is difficult to avoid the conclusions that the Conservative City editor uses the circumstances of a crisis to force the Government to bring in policies which he and his political friends think correct.

The fact is that the international financial community judges the relevance of Government action very largely on the views and opinions of the financial press in London. In the same way if the City page columnists *expect* an improvement in the monthly trade figures of £X millions – that is the standard by which the actual figures will be judged. And the City press – or a large part of it – must take the responsibility for putting pressure on the Government to adopt policies which it represents as the policies favoured by the financial markets. A less supine administration might have dared to challenge the 'accepted wisdom' of deflation, cuts in public expenditure, and statutory laws against the unions.

Headlines such as 'Bankers want tighter squeeze'; 'Market looks to Chancellor for cuts in welfare spending'; can all help to pre-limit the options of Government when facing crises. By raising expectations in the markets that certain policies must be followed, the press helps to ensure that they will be. Such research as has been done on this question indicates that the financial press attribute far more dogmatic policy opinions to the gnomes than they in fact possess.

A decade ago the influence of the City press was much more limited. Indeed it was barely possible until the late 1950s to speak of a City press. City and financial comment was typically restricted to a daily column of about 600 words; sometimes it appeared only two or three times a week. The City desk came low down in newspaper management's list of priorities for money and space allocation. 'The monthly gardening notes were thought to have more newspaper sex appeal and reader interest than anything we wrote,' was the way one retired City journalist put it to me. It was accepted that financial journalists were addressing themselves to a restricted readership; a coterie of financiers and investors. What the City institutions did or thought was held to be of no real interest to the non-investing public. In some cases this was accompanied by the view that popularizing the role of the City would be liable to stir up 'public prejudice and hostility'. This close identification between the financial writer and the City often went with a rigorous refusal by City writers to hold shares or have any financial interest in the companies about which they were likely to write.

Until recent years it was custom and practice among City journalists to accept 'official guidance' from the Treasury and the Bank of England when it came to interpretation of financial statistics. There is no doubt that this inhibited serious, critical journalism. Some City editors were little more than mouthpieces for the official and semi-official City institutions. There was a similarly respectful attitude displayed in the treatment of City news. Company directors, financiers and City traders were portrayed as essentially altruistic individuals. Rarely was there any hint of the venality, power politics and ruthless warfare which marks so much of the City's dealings. In this respect matters have clearly improved. There is little attempt today to represent the contestants in a takeover battle as anything other than wolves in wolves' clothing.

The revolution in popular financial journalism really dates from the period of the 1959 general election. At about that time two things dawned on both newspaper editors and proprietors; that there were both readers and lucrative advertising to be won by emancipating the City page Cinderellas. From that time on City editors could rely on their employers to treat their requests for money, space and other resources with favour. Almost overnight the status and influence of financial editors in the executive hierarchy of the daily newspaper was transformed.

The City page revolution was stimulated by several different factors. In the first place it was quite clear by the end of the 1950s that investment was becoming of interest to a wider range of people. The introduction of unit trust investment, in particular, helped to swell the ranks of the 'investing public'. It remained (and remains) true that a tiny proportion of the investors – less than five per cent – owned the great bulk of investment capital. But far more middle and lower middle class readers now took an interest in the City share markets and the factors which influenced it. The new readership was less interested in the esoteric accounts of high finance which characterized most City pages at that time. What they wanted were simply written accounts of what lay behind share movements on the market, changes in the economy and acts of Government which affected both.

The interest of this new readership was stimulated by introducing share tipping columns. Indeed the share tipsters approached their subject in much the same spirit as their racing colleagues.

These were the boom years on the stock exchange. Share values rose with barely a pause. The introduction of profitable private companies to the market and the explosion of takeover 'situations' all fed the increase in share prices. Tipsters could, but rarely did, go wrong. A further inducement to the new 'small' investor was the daily list of quoted share prices against which he could measure the rise in his holdings. By the early 1960s the popular press, as well as the more traditionally investment-minded 'heavies' could speak of a mass readership for their financial pages.

As a result City editors were able to persuade their editors and managements to allot them more money (for increased staff and production improvements) and for bigger, better paid staffs.

At the same time it became apparent that financial advertising was a major source of untapped revenue for the press. With more readers interested in investment and the fortunes of companies it was in the interests of companies to advertise their profit results and issue their comments on prospects. The boom markets also brought a flood of new private companies looking for share quotations. The advertising of prospectuses of companies about to be launched on the Stock Exchange brought in an increasing amount of advertising. At a later stage the expansion of unit trusts brought a further huge source of income. They in their turn were followed by the banks, insurance companies and building societies – all looking either for customers or investors' deposits.

The power of the financial advertisers is enormous. It is far more arbitrarily exercised than is true of general consumer advertising. Financial advertising goes through three lots of hands before it finds its way to the financial advertising manager in the newspaper City office. In the first place there is the company chairman or board of directors. When their company first comes to the market it is bound, by Stock Exchange ruling, to advertise the prospectus in two national papers.

There are no such regulations governing other forms of financial advertising. However, unit trust, banking, or insurance advertising is placed with some regard for the economic facts of life. Not so with the bulk of company chairmen's annual statements. One leading financial advertising agency executive puts it like this: 'The psychology of the chairman is often more important in deciding where his company's statement will appear than anything which either we or his financial advisers will say.' Political prejudice plays its part in allocating this type of advertising. Many chairmen have decidedly right-wing political views. As a result 'left of centre' papers tend to suffer. A minority of company executives make no secret of their prejudices. One titled chairman justifying his refusal to include the *Guardian* on his list of papers to carry his annual statement said: 'They advocate action against Smith in Rhodesia. We have factories in Rhodesia which Smith protects against a black takeover.' Many chairmen use the space bought by their companies on the City pages to launch openly political attacks on different aspects of Government policy, notably on taxation. Some financial advertising agencies emphasize the opportunities for 'pulpit preaching in the press' when encouraging companies to advertise their annual statements.

Most company chairmen leave the decision about financial PR in the hands of their merchant bank advisers. Political prejudice is not unknown in these bodies either. They tend to be less interested in the paper's circulation than whether the paper's readers 'are of a type to be interested in investment'. The banks in turn work with the financial advertising agencies who tend to be more professional and impartial. But even the agencies will not risk defying the known political prejudices of their principals by including 'suspect' papers on the list for advertising.

City journalists have to tolerate other forms of pressure from companies and their financial advisers. Many chairmen believe that their statements not only warrant advertising but editorial reporting as well. No matter how trite his sentiments or biased his judgment Mr X feels his views are news. And there is always the tendency to withdraw advertising if his company's results are not fully reported. It is a struggle for journalists to present a mass of financial and economic facts and figures in a readable and attractive manner. The lot of the City sub-editor is still more difficult if the pages are made up of columns of reports and comments of every minor company with a share quotation.

In the late 1950s financial advertising in the national press was probably not running at much more than £1 million. Today it totals around £10 millions a year. It has enabled the national press to increase the space coverage given to financial matters and to pay their staffs, by Fleet Street standards, very high salaries. Well into the 1960s there was a chronic shortage of journalists willing to work in the City. The old, fusty image stuck; in spite of the fact that promotion chances were far better in the financial pages than elsewhere. City editors found themselves obliged to poach each other's staff. At one stage it was not unknown for men to pass back and forth between two or three

newspapers – each time obtaining a substantial salary increase.
Today young men entering can expect to be paid 25 per cent
above the Fleet Street National Union of Journalists' minimum.
Some are paid starting salaries of between £1700 to £2000. Many
City editors today started little more than ten years ago as office
boys; few had university qualifications. Much to the chagrin of
their Fleet Street colleagues City editors tend to be paid second
only to the editor (and in some cases as much as the editor). Of
one City editor on a popular daily it is said, 'he talks only to
the managing director and will take instructions from no one
else'.

In spite of the enormous increase in advertising revenue, the
deteriorating economics of modern newspapers have made them
ever more dependent on this source of revenue. In recent years
easily obtained advertising has declined with the disappearance
of the boom in the share markets. Few new companies are coming
to the market and financial directors are seeking economies in
advertising outlays. The result is a further concentration of advertising in a few papers known for their investing readership. The
Financial Times and to a lesser extent the *Daily Telegraph* are
considered obligatory for financial advertising. In pursuit of
financial advertising *The Times* decided to publish its *Business
News*. So far this has proved a very expensive operation and there
is little sign that its costs are being covered by advertising revenue.
The *Daily Mail* has had rather more success with its 'Money Mail'.
However, the return of harder times has made the fight to win
City readers more important. From being the least news-conscious
sections of the national press the City columns are now among
the most sensational.

None of this is to deny that the serious dailies have surpassed
all previous standards in the way in which economic and financial
news and comment is presented. The *Financial Times* is out on
its own in this sphere and is rightly accorded an authoritative
status throughout the world. Both *The Times* and the *Guardian*
have undergone revolutions. The latter, within narrow budget
limits, has nonetheless helped to win a large slice of that paper's
growing readership. Although *The Times Business News* has not
yet covered its costs, it has added considerable prestige to the
paper as a whole, particularly through the standard of its economic
comment.

The high standards of this section of the financial press are
acknowledged by both Government and industry. The *Financial*

H

Times, *The Times* and the *Guardian* have all lost some of their most able young men either to industry or Government. Sir Gordon Newton, the editor of the *Financial Times* is credited with the remark that his paper was increasingly the 'University training ground for a new generation of business executives'. That paper has certainly lost more than a dozen of its brightest financial writers to executive positions in leading British companies like British Leyland and Courtaulds.

There has also been a steady flow of financial journalists to Government and semi-Government service. The Treasury, the Department of Economic Affairs, the Prices and Incomes Board, and the Industrial Re-organization Department have all benefited from recruitment among the ranks of City writers.

The picture in the popular press is not so happy. Although the serious press is not free from the pressures of the readership and advertising battle, the populars suffer to a more marked degree. The decline of the 'bull' market in shares has created problems for the 'pop' City editors. Share tipping is being gradually phased out of City columns, but not before confidence in the investment punditry of some of the City pages had been badly shaken. With the decline of big investment stories it is, perhaps, natural that the popular City pages should have turned more and more to national economic affairs to whet the appetites of their sensation-hungry readers. Yet it is in this field that some of the popular newspaper City pages have displayed the greatest irresponsibility.

There is a two-fold basis for the sensationalized and alarmist manner in which economic news is all too often presented in sections of the popular press. The first stems from the sheer technical difficulty of presenting complex economic facts and relationships. It is much easier to speak about Britain 'going broke' than to explain that while Britain is in debt to the international bankers, the value of share investments held by British citizens abroad exceeds the value of the country's official liabilities.

In the second place the popular press gives a quite exaggerated importance to the significance of rumour, particularly on the foreign exchange markets. The trouble is that these rumours, once repeated in the press, are read abroad by holders of sterling and are taken to reflect official opinion in Britain. What starts as speculation over the coffee break in a foreign exchange dealer's office, becomes 'reliable reports' when it is retold in the City columns, and reaches Zurich as 'fact'. When so much economic

news is gloomy this snowball movement can easily be started.
All too often the ominous expression 'City opinion' or 'the view
on the foreign exchange market' is an omnibus substitute for the
off-the-cuff remark made by one or more dealers in foreign curren-
cies. Dealers will readily speak to the press. The most accessible
are the relatively junior men. Their economic training is scant.
Yet their comment on frequently complex and involved figures
and economic statistics such as the trade figures or the balance of
payments can be the basis for sweeping judgments expressed on
the City pages. Exchange dealers, like brokers and other City
operators, are steeped in the political preconceptions and values
of the City. There is no real place for a Labour Government in
their scheme of things. Even a Government as right-wing and
appeasing of the City as Harold Wilson's. Yet their views get
publicized round the world. Can one blame the so-called gnomes
in Zurich and elsewhere for taking measures to protect their investments (even when the consequences are disastrous for sterling)
when the City's own opinions on the economic and financial
prospects can be so defeatist? Some City editors uninhibitedly
retail the prejudices of their contacts. There can be little doubt
that over a period such writing hastened the advent of devaluation.

The City editors of the *Daily Mail*, the *Evening News* and the
Sunday Express have all at different times made it clear in their
columns that there can be no lasting restoration of confidence in
sterling until a Tory Government is returned. Interestingly the
more thoughtful Conservative papers, such as the *Daily Telegraph*
and *Sunday Telegraph*, have been less partisan. And their city
editors have from time to time taken leave to question whether
the mere return of a Conservative Government would act like a
political stain remover.

Right-wing financial writers have also acted as a conveyor belt
of ideas and policies from the City to the Government. A full-
blown campaign has been waged in the past three years to persuade, bully and cajole the Government into believing that the
only salvation lay in dismantling the welfare state, slashing public
expenditure and granting tax relief to the higher-paid business
executives. This would not be too bad if it were not presented as
the views of our international creditors and the international
financial community. The suggestion has been made repeatedly
that only by carrying through such policies can the Government
ensure the continuing support of the bankers.

Of course it is true that sterling will be vulnerable for as long as there is a balance of payments deficit. It is also true that irrespective of the City press the world bankers have strange ideas on how to achieve balanced economic growth. It is true that without one City editor putting the idea into their heads, many of these bankers firmly hold to the view that Britain 'cannot afford' the welfare state or increasing state social expenditure. But the openly partisan polemics of an influential section of the financial press have lent much greater weight to these forces.

The anachronistic mechanism of the City places great power to influence the movement of sterling into the hands of the professional operators. By buying or selling sterling, sometimes ahead of the commercial requirements, these men can tip the balance against a given exchange rate. It is the dealers who are most influenced by the City press. And it is they who provide most of the economic 'interpretations' of the economy which is reported by the popular financial journalists. This incestuous relationship passes in many cases for valid economic journalism.

The danger is that with the continuing squeeze and every likelihood that financial advertising will get progressively harder to come by the temptation to win and hold readers by crude sensationalism will grow. Advertising revenue is showing alarming signs of concentration. The *Financial Times* and *Daily Telegraph* are getting by far the largest slice of financial advertising revenue. *The Times* is so worried about the situation that recently they decided to charge companies for what had, hitherto, been a free service to readers, the daily quotation of share prices. Some anger was caused in City circles, however, by *The Times* decision to remit the charge to those companies who undertook to advertise their chairman's statement and interim results. Some advertising men place their hopes in the council of the Stock Exchange making it obligatory for companies to advertise in a wider selection of newspapers. But there is no sign of this happening. The decline in revenue has not only been caused by the dearth of new companies coming to the market but also by the spate of mergers and takeovers which tends to reduce the number of public companies who need to advertise their results.

This worsening advertising situation is also not going to encourage editorial enterprise where this might offend a powerfully placed advertiser, or an institution responsible for drawing up the advertising schedules. The *Sunday Times* has been among the most courageous of papers when it has come to exposing stories on companies or financial practices. Significantly, however, this job has most often been done by the Insight team rather than the Business supplement.

The City press has sat on top of most financial scandals until they have exploded beneath them. The sanction of advertising withdrawal combines with the libel laws which are so heavily weighted in favour of the person or institution criticized, to make British financial journalism tame and pliant.

Sometimes there are cases where news stories which involve prominent business people are actually suppressed. The story of the battle between Mr Robert Maxwell's Pergamon Press and the American Leasco, which drew attention to the financial position of Pergamon subsidiaries, is an example. It was not until after the investigation made by the City takeover panel that anything like the facts were revealed. But, weeks before, a journalist on the staff of *The Times Business News* learned that Maxwell family trustees were selling Pergamon shares in large quantities. The editor of the *Business News* refused to print the story although its accuracy was not disputed. The information provided by the journalist was used by the City takeover panel. Other papers have been involved in similar situations. In almost every case the responsible editorial authorities have admitted that they were in part influenced by the difficulties which publishing the story would have for their financial advertising colleagues.

It is difficult to be optimistic when assessing the outlook for the financial press. The *Financial Times* and the *Daily Telegraph* look to have an assured future. The experiment with the *Business Times* has yet to prove itself. The future of the expanded *Guardian* City pages is tied up with that of the paper as a whole. However, few of the 'heavies' are likely to place their future at risk by developing the kind of campaign journalism which necessarily is bound to hurt important City interests; interests which influence the placing of financial advertising. The populars, on the other hand, appear to see no alternative but to scream louder and longer than their rivals to attract and hold reader attention. The standards of economic and financial comment are likely to suffer further in the process. In this respect the City pages reflect in an extreme form the general crisis of the British national daily press.

9

Reviews reviewed

D. A. N. JONES

Among the arts and entertainments which I have reviewed are these: ballet, books, circuses, jazz, movies, music, opera, painting, pop, radio, sculpture, television, theatre.

What odd categories. Why have jazz, music and pop been separated? Surely radio, television and books should be considered as 'media' rather than as arts and entertainments? What about the 'Art' column you get in so many journals, which deals with painting, sculpture and any object displayed in 'Art' exhibitions by people who used to be 'Art' students? Since singing and dancing occur in many of these art forms, should there not be a song reviewer and a dance reviewer? Should there not be a trained pedant to deal with historical accuracy, grammar, plagiarism, rules of counterpoint? Since these art-forms are frequently censored by private and public authorities, should there not be reviewers specializing in the censorable subjects – bodily functions, politics and religious belief?

My point is that the categories are fixed, not by the reviewer, but by editors and impresarios. Certain columns are allotted in journals for certain categories of art and entertainment. Publishers send free copies of their new books; theatre managers and concert promoters send free tickets; art-gallery directors invite the press to private views. The aim is to secure advertisement for a product or event – the best kind of advertisement, an appreciation by an independent (i.e. unbribed) person sufficiently interested and skilled to attract the attention of hundreds, thousands, millions of other people, so that they will witness the event or consume the product.

A distinction may be drawn between a reviewer and a critic. A reviewer does not choose what he writes about: he takes on anything offered. My own 'career' as a book-reviewer, since 1963, has been excellently described by Cyril Connolly in his 1938 treatise, *Enemies of Promise*. A youngish graduate writes a book. An editor asks him if he would like to contribute to the literary pages of a journal. A certain column is allotted:

> Suddenly his name appears under a pile of tomes of travel; the secrets of Maya jungles, Kenya game-wardens, and ricocheting American ladies are probed by him. In a year's time he will have qualified as a maid-of-all-work and be promoted to reviewing novels. . . . If he is complimentary and quotable he will be immortalized on the dust wrapper and find his name in print on the advertisements. And eight to ten novels a fortnight, sold as review copies, add to his wages.

I am not sure that novel-reviewing is necessarily a 'promotion' from the travel-book section nowadays. Travel-books command a higher price at the reviewers' bookshops (which pay half-price for almost any clean review copy) and are dispatched by editors to reviewers in larger quantities than are novels. Further, it is essential to read a novel right through, with care, before you can turn in a decent review; but you can make a perfectly respectable article out of half-a-dozen travel-books without close reading, since the majority of them are shapeless. Further, travel-books can increase a reviewer's information to the point that he becomes recognized as an expert. When I was employed as a political journalist on *Tribune*, I used the information gleaned from my travel-book column in the *New Statesman* to such effect that I was invited to contribute an essay on British Arabia in the *Socialist Register*.

Connolly is right to mock book-reviewing, and I join him, since it is easy to become conceited when practising this trade. Although it is, as Connolly says, 'a whole-time job with a half-time salary, a job in which the best of him is generally expended on the mediocre in others', the reviewer has a real influence on others' livelihood; and therefore he is often cosseted and wooed by publishers, managers and impresarios. The artists and entertainers whom he reviews are grateful or resentful. Serious scholars, the true critics, sometimes lose their tempers when they see us journalists writing too quickly, too grandly, about important subjects which we have only briefly considered. Dr Leavis has written sharply against those journalists, or journalizing dons, who 'mime a profundity of solemn doubt'. Our snap judgments, if delivered too pontifically, may be taken for gospel by naïve readers – and, in more immediate terms, may cost our subjects a lot of money.

The responsibility is even heavier when we deal with live entertainment and its executants. A reviewer cannot finally destroy good, lasting work by an author or composer; but he can damage the brief career of an actor or singer. In New York an absurd degree of attention is paid to theatre reviewers; even in London, with the increase of monopolization in the press and the commercial theatre, theatrical productions are becoming over-dependent on the most influential reviewers. The audiences may not be so sheeplike as their New York equivalent; but the financiers, especially the ticket-agencies, are sometimes too ready to close down an expensive show if it gets 'bad notices' – even from some fool in a bad temper.

Editors decide, under pressure and persuasion from reviewers and impresarios, what are the categories of entertainment to be covered. Theatre is an established category. A local newspaper is likely to give more space to a local theatrical production than to the latest films; readers, it is thought, will have heard about the films already, from the London-based national press. In the London papers there is a strongly-marked difference between the popular and quality journals. All carry theatre reviews, but for obvious reasons the popular papers give the London theatre less space than the qualities do. Readers of quality papers are more wealthy and, even if they live outside London, more mobile than the majority of the populars' readership. In between the two kinds of journal stands the halfway house of such papers as the *Daily Mail* and *Evening Standard*, where considerable effort is made to attract a well-to-do readership by offering news of expensive commodities, such as theatre performances. For the most part, though, popular newspapers necessarily devote more space to films than to theatre. As in everything else to do with journalism, the writer is enmeshed in a triangular drift-net, outspread by proprietors, advertisers and readers. The proprietor must be able to offer the advertisers a certain kind of 'readership'. Theatre-goers make a good 'readership' for a salesman of expensive goods.

A poorer class of reader, the large class which makes up an audience for almost nothing but television, is attractive to advertisers only when massed in huge numbers. Thus, it is well worth the proprietor's while to run reviews and features in the popular press about, say, Broadway export musicals, which are intended to run for a long time and attract poorer citizens in coach-loads for their rare outings.

This is where the popular papers' reviews become quite important, in commercial terms. Musical comedies are expensive to promote, and (unlike operas) unsubsidized. If the reviewers fail to lend support to the paid advertisements, if they decline to attract the readers' attention, then the ticket agencies will say: 'A bad press', and cease to finance the show. It will then fold – often to the annoyance of an un-influential quality reviewer like myself who may have thought it a good show to be recommended to his friends. With large investments, or gambles, like the promotion of musicals, the quality reviewer has very little commercial influence. Promoters of mass entertainments quite often cannot be bothered to invite the reviewers in the smaller-circulation qualities: they are after bigger game, like the *Daily Mirror* and *Daily Express*.

As years go by, quality papers – that is their editors and writers – begin to accept the idea that an entertainment, or sport, popular with 'the masses' is not necessarily devoid of quality. Films were eventually accepted in quality columns; so was jazz. More recently, television has come to take over a fair bit of space in the qualities (it is, of course, the most important item in the populars' cultural department). The latest arrival is pop music, a subject very difficult to write about without seeming vulgar and/or pompous. (A similar phenomenon may be observed in the qualities' efforts to review football.) Pop reviewers have not yet found an appropriate style; but there is no need to worry. Jazz reviewers faced a similar hurdle, and surmounted it.

Often minority art forms drop out of favour in the qualities: they are felt to be lacking in general interest. Ballet is a case in point; although its admirers are extremely enthusiastic, there are so many readers who are not interested in it at all that editors don't feel obliged to cover it. An editor supposes that most of his readers will take a mild interest, at least, in his theatre and film reviews; if he loses his reviewer in these fields, he will work hard to get a good new one. But if he loses his ballet reviewer he may sit around and wait for someone else to turn up. The same applies, to a lesser degree, with 'Art' and 'Music' (as traditionally defined – the events and products offered on the Wigmore Hall and Bond Street circuits). Being men with a literary bias, editors are commonly more interested in the drama, theatrical or cinematic, than they are in the visual and the musical. Perhaps they too readily attribute their own bias to their readership. But the main influence on their decisions about what should be reviewed is, surely, fashion – the editor's sense of the 'mood of the day'. Radio reviewing, for instance, has dropped out of favour. Radio is a medium, not an art-form; it is in the same position as 'Books', but there is no advertising revenue. Unlike television, it is not felt to be something that everybody needs to know about; unlike minority art-forms with precise boundaries (chamber music, ballet) it cannot command the services of a devoted pressure group.

This is only the beginning of an explanation of the traditional system for allotting space to the various accepted categories. Personally, I would like to change them all, so that reviewers could cut more freely across the boundaries; but that's by the way. I am trying to show that it is natural that in theatre reviewing, for instance, the *Sunday Times* and *Evening Standard* should print the most commercially influential reviews; the former has the largest circulation among the week-end quality papers, while the latter is the nearest we have to a quality evening paper. It is relevant that the *Evening Standard* devotes much space to reviews of new books; it is worth the publishers' while to advertise here. You may say that I am over-stressing the economic element in class division: books and theatre tickets are not particularly expensive commodities. Perhaps; but new books and new shows are gambles for the purchaser, and it is necessary (for a sensible man) to have a small surplus before investing. These commodities are for the comfortably-off, the secure classes, and the reviewers are their tipsters. But, for the *Daily Mirror*, a new Shakespeare production is not so much a subject for review – a description of the event for the benefit of potential audiences. It is more a matter of 'news value': for instance, an actress may appear nude, or a versatile actor familiar from some vulgar TV series may be playing King Lear.

The populars' treatment of arts and entertainments is very important to our society; but we will leave them now and concentrate on the qualities which, perhaps, have more influence on the actual *producers*, as distinct from the salesmen. The tradition in the journals is to keep reviews quite separate from the main business. The most formalized instance is the *New Statesman* pantomime horse, with politics at the front and 'culture' at the back. Reviewers, unlike political and industrial correspondents, are generally allowed an unusual degree of freedom to express their personal ideas about the great unmentionables – politics, religion and the bodily functions – without having to follow too closely 'editorial policy', the party line of the capitalist press. Thus journalists of left-wing opinion can make some kind of living in the review pages, where they are more or less tolerated.

One result of this established custom is that more conservative writers are enabled to spread (and believe) a myth that 'the press' is in the hands of the Left, or 'liberals', or 'so-called progressives', or 'Progs', or 'Lefties'. This myth is eloquently promulgated by single-minded anti-Communists, such as Kingsley Amis or Bernard Levin – men who are, perhaps, misinformed because they read the reviews section with more interest than the political section; men who find it quite natural that their own essays upon the state of the world should be welcomed in the front half of papers, but are alarmed to see dissenting opinions in the reviews.

It is still sometimes believed that it is possible to keep political opinions out of the review pages. This belief is most commonly brought up against the Leftward-leaning. A music or ballet reviewer is entitled to express the received opinions felt to be 'responsible' by the controllers of the British press; he may fulminate against the iniquity of the Russians in Czechoslovakia, he may sneer at Che Guevara as a kids' pin-up, he may mime a profundity of solemn doubt concerning American conduct of the war in Vietnam. But to be consistently Left of the editor's own opinions can be dangerous, and attract readers' complaints about political bias. It must be remembered that the majority of long-educated people vote Conservative. Politics of one kind or another is bound to obtrude into every kind of reviewing, and the reviewer's bias ought to be accepted and allowed for. Take two recent theatrical productions. Discussing an American show, the right-wing theatre reviewer of the *Financial Times* recently praised the Portuguese regime in Angola, comparing it admiringly with the old German regime in Togo. The liberal reviewer in *The Times* attacked Peter Terson's satire on student 'revolutionaries' for being 'right-wing suburbanite'. I don't agree with either of these opinions; but each of them has an arguable point, and they would not be reviewing the plays properly if they were discouraged from making those points.

When we turn to book-reviewing, obviously a political stance must sometimes be recognized as essential, by everyone. When I was assistant literary editor on the *New Statesman*, we had a deeply-committed opponent of the Soviet Union to review books about Russia and her European neighbours; we had books about China regularly reviewed by a man who was sympathetic to the Chinese Communist regime. A crazy policy, you may say; but both were well-informed, and good writers. When sub-editing this copy, for space or sense, I had to allow for my own political bias. Suppose the anti-Communist has, in my view, wrecked his own informed argument by overstatement and shrill rhetoric? My duty is to ensure that he publishes as good an article as possible. My inclination is to let him expose his own failings – and then have friends and readers cancelling their subscription, because they find our Russian expert offensive? Anyway, I could be wrong. Perhaps he is not being shrill, perhaps he is making a good point forcibly and I am blinded by prejudice. The best thing is to ring him up and ask him to suggest cuts. But we might not agree. He might want to cut out his 'good', informative stuff, and leave in the 'bad', rhetorical passages . . . I don't pretend this rather absurd problem crops up often when editing, not consciously anyway, but such considerations are often the basis, I believe, of snappy arguments between editors and reviewers.

Much of this is shadow-boxing – but may still be influential in the real world. After all, what is 'TV Violence' but shadow-boxing – and everyone's worried about that. Reviewers' shadow-boxing can make real things happen, or stop them happening. Some artists, though, complain that it's all fake, all mimed. Here is a passage from Doris Lessing's new novel, *The Four-Gated City*. (I take the quotation from D. J. Enright's review in the *New York Review of Books*. Enright says that these are 'sound remarks about the shadow-boxing of the British press and other mass media'.) Mrs Lessing's case is this: 'Apparently it was a scene of debate, competition, violently clashing interests . . . The newspapers that remained might call themselves right, left or liberal, but the people who wrote them were interchangeable, for these people wrote for them all at the same time, or in rapid succession. The same was true of television: the programmes had on them the labels of different companies, or institutions, but could not be told apart, for the same people organized and produced and wrote and acted in them. The same was true of the theatre. It was true of everything.'

A good many questions are begged here. But we will take D. J. Enright's comment: 'Including the literary columns: either you get reviewed by the whole metropolitan press or you get reviewed by none of it. For all the show of rivalry and independence of judgment etc., it's as if the editors have gone into a huddle to decide which new books to notice and how to notice them.'

Yes, the results are 'as if' that had happened. But there is no need, or little need, for a conspiracy theory except as a metaphor. The reviewers and editors of the different journals are the same kind of people and they behave alike. The more they work together, following the same kinds of routine, the more alike they become. They understand each other's language. (When Anthony Burgess remarked in a review of a novel of mine that it was 'literate, not to say literary', my aunt thought this was a compliment, and I knew it was a dig.) Reviewers form a recognizable sub-group with characteristics in common. Most of us are university graduates who retain the undergraduate habit of writing an essay every week, some sort of critical appreciation of another man's work. We are not merely being informative, like reporters; we are also offering a performance, as we were when studying for our exams – in competition with others. An editor cannot bear to see a book or play discussed in a rival journal and ignored by his own reviewer. 'Everybody's talking about it,' he may say, exaggerating. 'If it's no good, say why it's no good. You can't just ignore it.'

Commercial competition necessarily leads to a degree of conformity, even uniformity. The word goes round: 'Nobody goes to Edinburgh any more (or the Westminster, or the Unity). Everybody's going to the Living Theatre this week.' This is not a matter, as people in the provinces often suppose, of London cliques, claques and salons, deliberately planning a concerted attitude; that is as far-fetched as the idea of a capitalist plot, with millionaires gathered in a cellar to discuss means of doing down the working class, under the chairmanship of the very fat man who waters the workers' beer. The truth is, as we all know, that capitalists tend to do down the working class *accidentally*, in a spirit of enlightened self-interest. Similarly London editors and reviewers pass over the work of artists and entertainers with an unknown background, in favour of (let us say) some chap who was at college with a chap they know; or the son of a famous man; or the poems of a well-known novelist, on the ground that people will want to know what his poems are like, even if they're not much good. The snobbery involved is not generally recognized by those who practise it. Moreover, compensation is felt to be made when suddenly a whole non-graduate background is made fashionable: when, suddenly, every East End playwright (1950s) or photographer (1960s) is thought fit to be discussed, or every angry young 'Northerner' from Nottingham to Middlesbrough, or every little poetaster in the 'Liverpool Scene'.

During this century, the pattern of reviewers' shared conceptions has changed only through the arrival of fresher, younger men from the universities, with a new theory or a new working-class 'scene' to exploit. Sometimes they set up rival, little magazines against the established ones; nowadays these rival reviews are known as 'the Underground Press'. We may expect that the newcomers will wind up as editors of established journals – attracting advertisements for expensive commodities. The chances of my ever being enabled to attempt to review arts and entertainments intelligently for an interested working-class public in a successful journal are, to put it mildly, slim.

This does not mean that reviewers are necessarily a hindrance to the development of arts and entertainments. I believe we are often quite useful as interpreters between the workers in these fields and the 'public', the people who may accept the artists' work as treats for their leisure. I find reviewing, especially in the theatre, a most enjoyable occupation, the only disadvantage being that I get over-stimulated. Consider the bromides offered by television, and contrast with the live theatre where, at least once a week, I am seeing either an acknowledged masterpiece or a team of artists working themselves to death to persuade me that their ambitious piece will be recognized as a masterpiece one day. I am being educated and informed in a most congenial way. Yet, at the same time, I have to give a performance to make a living. Connolly offers sourly prudential advice: a reviewer should 'never write a review that cannot be reprinted, i.e. that is not of some length and on a subject of permanent value . . . neither will he spend himself on cheap subjects, nor put down his whole view of life in a footnote, for he will write only about what interests him.' He warns that the reviewer, 'besides losing the time to write books of his own, is also losing the energy and application, frittering it away on tripe and discovering that it is his flashiest efforts which receive most praise'. This is a good expression of *belles-lettristes'* melancholy; but I, for one, like these things the way they are: this situation in which 'a good review is only remembered for a fortnight; a reviewer has always to make his reputation afresh'. We are involved, in a small way, in making things happen *now*, in reacting as well as responding. As for posterity, some of our descendants may be interested in looking up old files, not in search of wisdom but to find out what we think *now* in 1970 – just as I now look up the theatre reviews of Hazlitt and Bernard Shaw and Antonio Gramsci and T. J. Wooller. This is quite good enough. There is no reason for reviewers to suppose that they are getting things right, at first sight, but no reason for them to despise themselves either. We are lucky fellows, having an easy time, doing no great harm.

If, in the interests of better reviewing, we want to change the conditions of our work, I can only suggest that here, as in all departments of journalism, there is need for at least some part of the press to be independent of advertising, and competition for advertising, and the conformity resulting from the need to appeal to the 'lowest common denominator' in a readership defined by 'income group'. To secure adequate broadcasting, theatre, opera and ballet, it has been found necessary to pay a public subsidy; and there is no reason why such a subsidy should not be paid for journals of reviewing, if the need is felt by the public. Another valuable reform would be a change in the law, or convention, about damaging people's livelihood, so that reviewers may be permitted to criticize publishers, impresarios and managers as severely as we may criticize artists and entertainers.

This may seem a minor point, but it is important to those of us who want to see the great halls and theatres and galleries of Britain eventually made public, under democratic control. In the meantime the capitalists who control them ought to be criticized, to be praised or blamed. For instance, I wanted to see *Soldiers*, Hochhuth's frightful play about Churchill. Note, first: I can safely write 'frightful' about an artist's work, not about a businessman's. Next: I can safely criticize Victor Mishcon (for whom I have voted and, as it happens, canvassed) who was the Greater London Council representative on the National Theatre board: I think he was wrong to vote against the National Theatre's production of *Soldiers*. But can I safely criticize Bernard Delfont for refusing to accept the play in his privately-owned theatres? He might prove to be as litigious as Tycoon X.

I once publicly criticized Sidney Bernstein, the sultan of

Granada, for allowing his London cinemas to degenerate into 'bingo-holes and wrestling-pits': he wrote to me, listing in some detail the valuable examples of art and entertainment which had appeared in his cinemas during recent months. He explained that he did not want a public apology: he wanted me, as a journalist, to know the true facts. If all tycoons were equally sensible, we would be enabled to criticize the *controllers* of the media as fairly as we try to criticize the workers, without being pestered by the lawyers – legal advisers, libel experts and the idolized judiciary.

10

Fringe press and naked emperor

PETER FRYER

He is a brave or reckless man who undertakes to write on the fringe press. For one thing, fringe editors are sometimes touchy about criticism, even when it is constructive and good-natured. A couple of years ago, some well-meaning remarks of mine about the hippy newspaper *International Times* – since officially renamed *IT* – made its then editor, a rather anxious American expatriate, very cross indeed. All I had done was mention *IT*'s indifference to accepted canons of journalism, its not seeming to mind whether the customers could actually read those fragmented, upside-down or sideways-on items with their curving lines of type, their generous scatterings of literals and 'doublers'. *IT*'s strivings to burst its banks, as it were, to become something more than a mere newspaper, to be a series of mind-blowing posters, a game, a toy, and a talisman as well – these strivings I had taken to be purposeful, sharply distinguishing the organ of the turned-on under-thirties from all overground, pre-McLuhan journals. I thought it was *meant* to be slovenly and amateurish.

Again, there is a major problem of definition and selection to be coped with. 'Fringe press' is clearly not the ideal way of describing the newspapers or anti-newspapers in question. Independent, anti-Establishment, iconoclastic, more or less left-wing, more or less revolutionary: this intolerable mouthful sums up more accurately the common ground these periodicals stand on. Even then, there are important differences among them. The word 'revolutionary' would undoubtedly be interpreted differently

I

by each; *IT*, for example, has always steered as clear of politics, especially violent politics, as an obstinately political and violent world would permit. Perhaps the term 'free press' is the least unsatisfactory. These papers are free from press lords, free from rich advertisers and their influence, and free from too crippling a regard for the laws concerning sedition, obscenity, and libel.

Two papers I used to work for are omitted from this survey – not because I used to work for them (though that might well alloy my objectivity) but rather because neither of them, despite bold claims, is independent or iconoclastic or revolutionary in anything like the ways the others are. Their irreverence towards existing institutions, for instance, is highly selective. To be sure, the *Morning Star* has lately ventured to disagree with Soviet policy towards Czechoslovakia.

A similar limitation impairs the claim of the infant *Workers Press* – whose immediate predecessor *The Newsletter* I had the doubtful honour of founding in 1957 – to be included among the free press as here understood. Originally intended as a newsletter for those who quit the British Communist Party after the 1956 Hungarian Revolution, *The Newsletter* long ago ceased even pretending to be a news-sheet. Instead it preferred to lead its readers, step by step, through the barren fields of Trotskyist heresy-hunting. The *Workers Press* has inherited *The Newsletter*'s singular preoccupation with enemies and traitors, including the 'rat groups', as rival organizations on the far left used to be known in the S.L.L. Costing sixpence per issue, it claims to be 'the daily organ of the Central Committee of the Socialist Labour League'; in fact it appears five times a week. Even so, its production and independent distribution must put a colossal strain on the S.L.L.'s meagre resources. Its publication is a considerable achievement, attributable more to commercial acumen and long hours of work than to political successes of any kind.

Then there are several journals which, logically speaking, should be included but are clearly of far less consequence than their rivals, and are likely to remain so. *Peace News*, for instance, was once a force to be reckoned with. But it made the mistake of tying its fortunes too closely to the Committee of 100, and when that phase of the anti-bomb movement was superseded, *Peace News* found itself left behind. Changes for the worse in format, an eccentric and unenticing title-piece, a price increase to a shilling a copy, and editorial enthusiasm for anarchist doctrines all helped to lose readers; the new readers whom this latter development might have been expected to attract were already being served by other journals. The future of *Peace News* is clearly uncertain.

The *Socialist Worker* ('For workers' control and international socialism'), a threepenny weekly produced by the group of Trotskyists, or neo-Trotskyists, around *International Socialism*, is not merely earnest but surprisingly dull for a paper written and distributed by young people. Dullness is no longer an inevitable by-product of political dedication, and a paper whose contributors include Paul Foot, Nigel Harris, and Peter Sedgwick ought to be far livelier than it is. Perhaps its main trouble is being too parochial (front page item, in full: '*Socialist Worker* congratulates John and Jenny Southgate on the birth of their first son, Leon').

Solidarity (originally *Agitator*), which appears irregularly, specializes in detailed and informative accounts of industrial disputes, written with obvious inside knowledge and always from the point of view of the man at the workbench. The flavour is often reminiscent of those first-hand accounts of workshop conditions that used to appear in the 1930s *Left Review*. *Solidarity's* chief handicap is that it is duplicated, not printed, and this cannot but reduce its influence. Otherwise, with its refreshing irreverence towards all established institutions and political organizations, it would have gained much more support among those 'new layers' of youth and students that have become 'politicalized' in the last two or three years.

Fugitive papers, appearing for an issue or two and disappearing without a trace, have always been a feature of the extreme left, and never more so than today. Their ephemerality, which is of their essence, makes it hard to keep track of them. The British Situationists' *Heatwave* (two issues) is now a collector's item, as is the neo-nihilist, quasi-surrealist *King Mob*. Desmond Jeffery, who teaches at the London School of Printing, is responsible for the beautifully designed *Red Papers*, a cross between a newspaper, a poster, and a poem. Outside London, there are school papers like the Leeds *Hod*, banned by outraged headmasters because of features on 'Sex and Fascism' and 'Hendrix Blows a Mind', the use of four-letter words, and 'invitations to meetings in what appeared to be rather sordid surroundings'. *The 1/- Paper*, produced by a group of Cambridge undergraduates and claiming a circulation of 2,000 copies a week, scored by reproducing a letter sent by an official at the War Office to about twenty students, asking them 'to assist this department in a current project we have in mind' and not to tell anyone about it. (The secret project turned out to be the provision of occasional reports on certain students' political activities and attitudes.) Other university free papers include Brighton's *Mole* and Manchester's *Grass Eye*.

The inspiration behind free journalism at the universities seems to have been the unexpected but undeniable success of the *Black Dwarf*. Originally conceived as a magazine, it was launched as a newspaper on the insistence of Christopher Logue. Most other supporters, and opponents, were less confident of its success in this format; but the hurried remaking of the inaugural issue after a last-minute dispute among the editors, a well-publicized police raid, and a series of vexatious difficulties with printers all seem to have helped rather than hindered the *Dwarf* in getting off the ground. The *Black Dwarf* is officially the direct continuation of T. J. Wooler's radical paper of the same name, and its title-piece carries the saucy claim: 'Established 1817'. What Wooler would have made of his continuers is anybody's guess; but the old *Black Dwarf* and the other radical papers of the day proudly adopted the hostile epithet 'two-penny trash', and the new *Black Dwarf* is no less gratified when its numerous enemies call it names. At all events, a circulation of 8,000 (sometimes rising to 10,000) and an estimated readership of 30,000, sixteen months after the first issue appeared, show that Logue's confidence was justified. It has been hard work achieving this circulation. Distribution problems are a major headache, since even independent newsagents willing to display *IT* and *Private Eye* look askance at a front-page call to revolution, or a picture of a Milan policeman kicking a student demonstrator in the testicles. The editors are convinced that a demand exists for the paper which is not being met and, as proof of this, they point to the ease with which it can be sold along youthful cinema queues.

The *Black Dwarf*'s main advantage over its political rivals is that it is not the mouthpiece of any organization, and is therefore committed to no 'line' laid down by a party or sect. It aims to be a non-sectarian revolutionary paper, 'a vanguard paper of the revolutionary left', and its columns have always been open to rank-and-file controversy. The exact balance to be drawn between readability and revolutionism has sometimes led to less publicized disagreements at the top; and one cannot but regret that Douglas Gill, who edited five or six issues with considerable flair, broke with the paper because of differences on both policy and layout. Again and again, in different guises, the problem of what to write about faces the *Black Dwarf*'s editors. How far, for instance,

should the paper take cognizance of the 'official' world it con-
demns and despises? Should the books of capitalist publishers be
reviewed? Should there be theatre and cinema notices? Or should
the paper mirror only the subculture of agitprop, the aesthetic
preoccupations of revolutionary activists? Not least, what attitude
should it take when the next general election arrives? Since there
is no 'line', the time comes when discussion must stop and a
decision must be taken, and it rarely satisfies every one of the
paper's friends and supporters. But the advantages of running the
paper as a political alliance – of people with a shared fundamental
outlook but with different views on secondary questions – are
thought to far outweigh the disadvantages.

In the event, the *Black Dwarf* has exemplified – whether deliberately or not, it is hard to say – Lenin's classic description of a
revolutionary newspaper as collective propagandist, collective
agitator, and collective organizer. Especially the latter. Much of
the success, in numerical terms, of the controversial London
demonstrations against the Vietnam war was due to its mobiliza-
tion of its readers. The issue immediately before the demonstration
of 27 October 1968, contained notes on 'what to do if you are
arrested', a piece by 'Fred Engels' on street fighting, and the
words of the Rolling Stones' song 'Street Fighting Man' (banned
by British record companies) written out in Mick Jagger's own
hand:

> Everywhere I hear the sound of marching, charging feet, boy
> Cause summer's here and the time is right for fighting in the
> street, boy.

The *Dwarf* is proud of its 'crudely aggressive, brash and
optimistic political image', of its audacity and vulgarity. It sets
out deliberately, says Tariq Ali, to 'offend bourgeois sensibilities'
by insulting its enemies. This is a question of political style. The
widespread frustration among the under-thirties, their disillusion-
ment with politics, including traditional left-wing politics, means
that young people will no longer listen to political agitation
couched in drawing-room language. The rapier has gone into cold
storage for the time being, and the bludgeon has taken its place.
A thug is called a thug, and the *Dwarf* has been specially outspoken about the murky private armies used to evict squatters;
about a police officer against whom it is alleged that he has not
always helped foster good race relations in north Kensington;
about the furtive activities of Scotland Yard's Special Branch, or

political police, who keep tabs on left-wing organizations and publications, and are frequent visitors to the *Dwarf* offices; about Mr Enoch Powell; and about some of his keenest supporters – the 'skinheads', the lumpenproletarian youths who remain obstinately unimpressed by, and inarticulately resentful of, the hippies and lefties among their contemporaries.

But there is much more in the *Black Dwarf* than name-calling, police-baiting, and such. I can think of no socialist periodical in Britain that has ever discussed the 'woman question' one-tenth so seriously. One thinks in particular of an editorial (10 January 1969) which had something new and mature to say about 'the changes in sexual patterns among the young in modern industrial society' and 'the revolutionary possibilities of a liberated and responsible sexuality', and which condemned the traditional left's 'puritanical and repressed view of the world'. To the *Black Dwarf*, women are human beings, and too many men are male supremacists, and to devote a good deal of space to women's liberation not only is correct in principle but also, as the editor and nominal proprietor Clive Goodwin puts it, wins support for the paper from the many 'angry young left-wing women' who are no longer prepared to be second-class citizens inside, or outside, the revolutionary movement. Female readers are advised on contraception and abortion, and unmarried mothers are warned to insist on their rights:

> In dealing with NAB officers you have to be prepared for anything . . . Be sure to know exactly how much the allowances are because they will try and fob you off with less.

Goodwin and his twelve colleagues on the *ad hoc* committee that runs the *Dwarf* are pretty frank about their problems and their shortcomings. Thus, though each issue carries industrial news, the paper has no industrial correspondent, and there is a shrieking absence of industrial workers from the committee. Many of the acknowledged weaknesses can be attributed to chronic shortage of money. The paper loses about £100 an issue. So far, a 'fairy godmother' has always come forward to pay the bills, and there is a young woman in Wales who has donated all of £1,500, to be repaid 'when the revolution comes'.

A strange relationship of rivalry-within-solidarity, or the other way round, subsists between the *Black Dwarf* and the 'underground' newspaper *IT*. Their street-sellers sometimes stand side by side, which is probably helpful in dealing with police harassment. On many questions – police treatment of young people is one – the two papers' interests and general policy coincide or overlap. But *IT* is a revolutionary paper in a special sense only: the revolution it conceives itself to be fostering is supposed to have taken place, or to be taking place, or to be going to take place, inside people's heads. One obvious watershed dividing the two papers' catchment areas is their readers' attitudes to cannabis. To the *Black Dwarf*, while 'pot is here to stay', the 'awful ageing truth' about it is that 'it isn't very important'. To *IT*, the subject is important enough to warrant occasional reports on current market prices per ounce of hashish smuggled into the country from Pakistan, the Lebanon, and elsewhere, as well as pieces like George Andrews's ecstatic account of how

> I've stayed high night and day for 22 years, out of my
> skull around the clock on the strongest charge in town, and
> am in better health than when I started.

But to dismiss *IT*, as many do, as the house organ of users of illegal drugs, or as 'the flower children's comic', is totally to misconceive the appeal it has for the 43,000 who buy it every fortnight. So large a circulation for a paper that most people over thirty tend to dismiss as bizarre and incomprehensible cannot be explained, either, by its notorious sex ads (now greatly toned down, though still soliciting 'broadminded' girls willing to correspond with 'uninhibited' men, and offering 'free Introductions for all Couples requiring Troilism this month . . . usual cheap rates for bisexual Individuals'); or by the celebrated photograph of a human female engaging, or appearing to engage, in sexual activity with a canine male; or by the recent detailed and quite horrifying account of John Fare's self-mutilation, reprinted from *The Insect Trust Gazette*; or by the hardly less disturbing reference to the two young women in Chicago whose hobby is making plaster casts of pop musicians' penes. There is plenty of sensational material of this kind, and it probably helps to keep *IT* popular with elderly smut-hunters eager to pay inflated sums for the paper's early issues. On the other side of the generation gap, *IT* is accepted for a very simple reason: its anti-authoritarian approach to everything faithfully reflects the attitude of most of its readers. It is written in a language they understand and use; it gives them a sense of belonging, to the 'tribe', or the 'community', or the 'supplementary society'; it discusses the music they adore at enormous length and, on the whole, pretty intelligently. In short, they find

128 *Peter Fryer*

themselves mirrored in its pages – and if their loyalty to it is narcissistic, this is a weakness they share with readers of, say, the *Daily Express* and *The Lady*.

IT has passed, in its brief career, through three fairly well-defined phases. In the first ten issues, edited by Tom McGrath, the text was intended, on the whole, to be read and was often well worth reading.

Then there came the police raid of March 1967, to which *IT* reacted with some degree of hysteria. A series of virtually unreadable issues called on kids to turn on their parents if they couldn't turn them on; some well-known names disappeared from its columns; the paper seemed to be set up and made up by a one-handed blind compositor. Both form and content improved gradually, and the paper assumed its present shape by about the middle of 1968.

In all fairness, it should be added that those who have kept *IT* going have had more than their share of police interference and trouble with printers. The present printer is the seventh in three years. Some of his predecessors chose to throw up the job at the last minute, when an issue was set up and ready to run off. One printer demanded a libel insurance policy, then (it is alleged) destroyed negatives and plates. One friendly printer, whose machines were unsuitable for *IT*, telephoned another printer to ask if he could handle the job. The reply was no, because 'the word is out'. Nevertheless *IT* completed, in the autumn of 1969, three years of unbroken publication.

IT's editors regard it, above all, as a sounding-board for what they call 'alternatives' – alternative life styles, forms of social organization, and so on – in a society which, as they see it, does not work very well and is not likely to improve very much. Most other papers accept the *status quo*, even if they pretend not to. *IT* is the voice of the youngster who resents and rejects the admonitions of headmasters, employers, trade union bosses, politicians, and advertisers. *IT* talks to its readers publicly exactly as they talk to each other in private: frankly, mockingly, self-mockingly, but with some regard for individual human beings and their rights. Other papers, *IT*'s staff argue, are in practice either consciously hypocritical or schizoid: their journalists say privately what they would never dare, or never be permitted, to print. Therefore *IT* goes on plugging its basic message: if the older generation, or most of them, have forgotten how to live, too bad; the younger generation have not forgotten, and do not intend to.

Over-thirties who have not forgotten, at any rate, how to laugh are among the devoted readers of *Private Eye*, which began life in 1962 as 'a fortnightly lampoon'. *Private Eye* developed out of the university journalism of Adrian Berry, whose *Parson's Pleasure*, parochial and pungent, brightened the Oxford scene at the end of the 1950s. After Berry, Paul Foot and Richard Ingrams (now *Private Eye*'s editor) edited *Parson's Pleasure* for a time, and a little useful practice was gained in the art of apologizing to people who were offended by what was written about them. Since 1966 *Private Eye* has apologized to Messrs John C. McGrath, John Stonehouse, John Monks, Elkan Allan, Derek Marks, Rodney Bennett-England, Jeremy Potter, Ian McColl, Ian Brown, John Gordon, John McCormick, Ian Sharp, Clive Irving, Robert Mellish, Sidney L. Bernstein, G. W. Rowe, Robert Maxwell, and others.

Private Eye's success depends on a skilful combination, infinitely less amateurish and accidental than it appears at first sight, of fifth-form insults and inside stories too hot for the unfree press to handle even if they wanted to. Schoolboy humour is a matter of taste, but there are evidently a good many people so fed up with politicians of every shade that they lap up references to '"Smoothiechops" Jenkins' and 'H. Wilsundra'; who are bored by the royal family and enjoy seeing its residual pomposity pricked; who enjoy the imbecilities that otherwise intelligent newspaper editors tend to incorporate into their internal memoranda; who, in a word, rejoice to see hypocrisy anatomized and cant deflated. No paper has done more than *Private Eye* to rehabilitate ridicule as a weapon of political and social criticism in this country. This helps to explain the disproportionate venom with which some of its victims have reacted, and their strong but hardly realizable desire to prevent this scurrilous rag from ever referring to them at all. It is annoying to be libelled; to be laughed at is a thousand times less bearable.

And, in truth, what other paper is so consistently funny as *Private Eye* has managed to be, as its sharp little nails have scratched, fortnight after fortnight, at the nation's piles? What other periodical has eyes so vigilant that it picks up, from far-off Bangkok, this 'headline of the year': 'Woman Dies of Diarrhoea after Attack by Owl'? What other paper would have dared blurt out the open secret about *Punch*'s prick, or reveal the BBC instruction that copulating animals must not be shown on television between the hours of six and seven in the evening? Or devote the cover of its first issue in 1969 to a picture of de Gaulle wishing 'a happy *soixante-neuf* to you all'? Or print the first of Mr William Rees-Mogg's memoranda on style, addressed to the staff writers of *The Times*: ' "Consensus" is an odious word. It is never to be used and when it is used it should be spelt correctly'?

But *Private Eye* not only makes its readers laugh; it also makes them think. By muckraking, of course; but muckraking is a perfectly honourable and worthy activity in a society where certain sorts of muck are regularly, and for the most part unquestioningly, swept under the carpet. Many of *Private Eye*'s best scoops have been stories that other papers knew about but chose to suppress. In 1964 it was the first to print the names of Ronald and Reginald Kray; *The People* followed suit eleven days later. *Private Eye* revealed that a number of Glasgow students had been suspended for alleged obscene telephone calls. It was the first to detail the background of Dr Walter Adams when he was appointed LSE principal. It gave the inside story of the affairs of Yorkshire Television, and revealed that the BBC spends an estimated £250,000 a year on taxis. It exposed the conditions inside Durham jail. It alone was bold enough to mention, and ask questions about, the secret 'Bilderberg Conference' held annually at St John's College, Cambridge. It scooped the rest of the press on the Hanratty case. Apart from *IT*, *Private Eye* alone revealed how a *News of the World* reporter had offered to buy Michael de Freitas an arms cache, so that a sensational story could be written about British adherents of the black power movement. *Private Eye* told the truth about the Porton Down germ warfare establishment. Its readers knew about the war in Nigeria long before readers of other papers. It was the first to give details about the scientologists' organization and its curious attitude to ex-members. It ran the inside story of 'Mad Mitch' and the Argylls in Aden. It gave the first and best account of the background to the Ronan Point disaster. It forecast the appointment of Chichester-Clark as Prime Minister of Northern Ireland. And it keeps a vigilant public eye on the activities of the National Front.

This is a record, whatever else one cares to say about it, of sheer professionalism – and it has done more than anything else to raise *Private Eye*'s circulation to 48,000. *Private Eye* is a constant uncomfortable reminder to a dwindling Fleet Street that skilled journalism is not men writing fatter cheques than their competitors, but men going to greater pains, finding out more, and having the guts to print the truth.

By far the oldest free paper in Britain is the anarchist weekly,

Freedom. Ten years ago it was also one of the least important, with a circulation under 2,000 and contents as hard to digest as a plateful of Bakunin's beard. No one seems to know exactly why, but the circulation is now about 4,000; if, as is sometimes said, this increase is due to a growing interest in anarchist theory and practice, how is one to explain the failure of the magazine *Anarchy* – on the whole more profound, better written, and more interesting – to win more readers in the same period?

My own hypothesis, for what it is worth, is that *Freedom* represents the condition the free press tends towards, without ever in practice attaining it. In other words, free papers tend in practice to adopt, spontaneously or at the most semi-consciously, a set of attitudes which, in terms of current politics, have much in common with traditional anarchist attitudes. They find it possible to do so even within a generally Marxist framework; one of the oddest, yet most significant, aspects of the sixties has been the emergence of various amalgams of anarchism and Marxism. Situationism is perhaps the best-known example. To an earlier generation of revolutionaries, such developments seem as outlandish as the hippogriff. But most young revolutionaries are cheerfully eclectic. And a minority of *IT* readers or *Black Dwarf* readers or other student activists, having become, as it were, neo-anarchists without realizing it, are tending to find in *Freedom* a more satisfying explanation of what they are doing, and trying to do, than they can find anywhere else.

For *Freedom* represents the ultimate in free papers: a searing weekly critique of practically everything, including anarchists themselves. This is one paper that makes no concessions whatever. It is serious, dedicated, scurrilous, and increasingly influential.

But then, the free press as a whole is becoming increasingly influential. This is probably inevitable in a society which purports to be democratic, but in which people feel increasingly cut off from decision-making. It would be idle to deny that free papers are childish. They print words like 'turd' and 'fart' in big letters and feel that they are thereby striking shrewd blows for freedom. But this is the least important thing about them. Their very childishness plays also a socially useful – I would say, an indispensable – role. In their different ways, and with their different emphases, they are crying out that the emperor is naked. This 'shit-stirring', this blurting out of disturbing and unseemly truths, this encouragement of heresy, is one of the few remaining barriers against the standardization and computerization of our lives.

11

Provincial press: towards one big shopper

A. C. H. SMITH

> Have you heard about Henry Luce's flop in Los Angeles? . . . He
> thought he could go around and buy up all the community news-
> papers out there and make one big shopper out of it. Well, when
> he did that the paper ceased being a community newspaper and
> he soon had to call it quits.[1]

Fifty years ago the circulation of daily newspapers published in
the provinces outnumbered that of London dailies by about a
third. Today, the London nationals have almost two-thirds of
the daily circulation. In addition, nearly half the provincial circulation (4·4 million of just under 9 million) is now controlled by
groups associated with the national press (see Table). One way of
representing these facts is to say that in comparison with London's
voice the independent provincial voice is now only one-seventh
as loud as it was. *1969*

That diminished voice is further restricted by the growth of
other large groupings with no national-paper association. The
largest of these holdings, United Newspapers' total circulation of
970,000, is also shown in the table. Other groups control the
Portsmouth Evening News, *Sunderland Echo* and *Northern Daily
Mail* (226,000); the *Southern Evening Echo*, *Dorset Evening Echo*
and *Bournemouth Evening Echo* (185,000); and, the George Outram
group, the *Glasgow Evening Times*, *Glasgow Herald* and *Paisley
Daily Express* (299,000).

[1] A Chicago community newspaper publisher quoted by Morris
Janowitz in *The Community Press in an Urban Setting* (New York:
Free Press, Glencoe, 1952).

Of the 75 evening papers published in the provinces (total circulation 6,994,000)[1] only Glasgow has two. Of the 20 morning papers (1,982,000) fifteen are grouped with the sole evening paper published in the same place. In Darlington, Plymouth, Newcastle, Leeds, Sheffield, Cardiff, Edinburgh and Aberdeen, the morning and evening papers both, as the table shows, belong to the same wider groupings; in Bristol, Liverpool, Birmingham, Nottingham, Norwich, Ipswich and Dundee, the morning and evening papers are owned by a single city-group. In Leamington Spa, where the tiny (12,000) *Morning News* is published, there is no evening paper. Thus only in Glasgow, where one Outram paper competes with the IPC in the morning and the other with the Beaverbrook Press in the evening, and in Belfast, where both morning papers are independent, are rival newspapers published in the same town.

Of the smallest-circulation papers, those published weekly or twice-weekly (163 of them in greater London, 995 elsewhere), about a quarter are owned by the big groups. More than 60 are controlled by the Westminster Press, and Thomson, Associated Newspapers and United Newspapers have 20 to 30 each. The majority are strung together in smaller local series, and still owned by family firms.

Since the late 1920s, when the first Lord Rothermere and the Berry Brothers carried their circulation battle beyond Fleet Street and pitched camps in the provinces, the process of grouping has not let up. The groups' concentrated siege on local sales and advertising has killed off independent papers by the score.[2] There are signs that the long contraction of titles may be ending, by courtesy of the big groups, who are slotting new papers into towns which are on the fringe of existing circulation areas and therefore not fully cropped of advertising. Five of the Thomson evening papers – in Reading, Burnley, Luton, Watford and Slough – date from the later 1960s, as does the Chatham evening paper, owned by a Kent group. At the time of writing the Westminster Press is planning a new evening paper in Southend, and a Surrey group has given a trial run to a new evening paper in Guildford. Most of these are ringed around London, to exploit the metropolitan evening

---

[1] Figures aggregated as total circulations are those given in the 1969 *Newspaper Press Directory*, except in a few cases of papers whose sale is not stated there but who supplied figures privately.

[2] A transient exception was the Westminster Press between the wars when, in its then Liberal policy, it rescued a number of drowning Liberal papers in the provinces.

Group control of Provincial daily newspapers

Group	Associated nationals	Provincial papers m = morning paper e = evening paper	Circulation in thousands
Thomson	*The Times*	m Newcastle *Journal*	115
Organization	*Sunday Times*	e Newcastle *Evening Chronicle*	250
		m Cardiff *Western Mail*	101
4 morning		e Cardiff *South Wales Echo*	150
12 evening[1]		m Edinburgh *Scotsman*	74
		e Edinburgh *Evening News*	158
		m Aberdeen *Press & Journal*	103
		e Aberdeen *Evening Express*	74
		e Belfast *Telegraph*	214
		e Teesside *Evening Gazette*	120
		e Blackburn *Lancashire Evening Telegraph*	72
		e Reading *Evening Post*	47
		e Burnley *Evening Star*	30
		e Luton *Bedfordshire Evening Post*	36
		e Watford *Evening Echo*	32
		e Slough *Evening Mail*	23[2]
		Total	1599
Associated	*Daily Mail*	m Plymouth *Western Morning News*	71
Newspapers	*Daily Sketch*	e Plymouth *Western Evening Herald*	69
	Evening News	e Derby *Evening Telegraph*	98
1 morning		e Exeter *Express & Echo*	39
12 evening		e Torquay *Herald Express*	25
		e Gloucester *Citizen*	40
		e Cheltenham *Gloucestershire Echo*	35
		e Leicester *Mercury*	180
		e Grimsby/Scunthorpe *Evening Telegraph*	73
		e Lincoln *Echo*	37
		e Stoke *Evening Sentinel*	125
		e Hull *Daily Mail*	133
		e Swansea *South Wales Evening Post*	71
		Total	996
United		m Sheffield *Morning Telegraph*	67
Newspapers		e Sheffield *Star*	205

Group control of Provincial daily newspapers

		m Leeds *Yorkshire Post*	118
2 morning		e Leeds *Yorkshire Evening Post*	261
6 evening		e Preston/Wigan *Lancashire Evening Post*	150
		e Blackpool *West Lancashire Evening Gazette*	78
		e Northampton *Chronicle & Echo*	56
		e Doncaster *Evening Post*	35
		Total	970
Westminster	*Financial Times*	m Darlington *Northern Echo*	116
Press		e Darlington *Northern Despatch*	23
		e South Shields *Gazette*	37
1 morning		e Barrow *North Western Evening Mail*	30
9 evening		e Oxford *Mail*	44
		e Bath *Bath & Wilts Evening Chronicle*	33
		e Brighton/Hastings *Evening Argus*	101
		e Swindon *Evening Advertiser*	34
		e Bradford *Telegraph & Argus*	126
		e York *Evening Press*	60
		Total	604
I.P.C.	*Daily Mirror*	m Glasgow *Daily Record*	527
	Sun		
	Sunday Mirror		
	People		
North News	*Guardian*	e Manchester *Evening News*	466
Beaverbrook	*Daily Express*	e Glasgow *Evening Citizen*	191
Press	*Sunday Express*		
	Evening Standard		
News of the	*News of the World*	e Hereford *Evening News*	} 41
World		e Worcester *Evening News*	
Organization			

Note The table covers England, Wales, Scotland and Northern Ireland, but not Eire. Circulations are as given in the 1969 *Newspaper Press Directory*, rounded to nearest thousand.

[1] The Manchester *Sporting Chronicle*, a Thomson morning paper with 89,000 circulation, has been omitted as too specialized in relation to this chapter.

[2] Circulation of Slough *Evening Mail*, which began publishing in 1969, is not officially audited but supplied on request.

papers' weakness in outlying areas, where they are slower with the news and too big to catch much local small advertising. The national morning papers, in contrast, distributed from London and elsewhere by overnight train, can reach virtually every home in time for breakfast. Although 20 provincial morning papers survive, it is here that the brunt of London's imperialism has been taken, and there is little chance that any new provincial morning could find enough advertising of the kind morning papers depend on.

Lord Thomson rejects the notion that chain-ownership need affect the character of newspapers. No Thomson editor anywhere in the world is told what policy to follow. Apart, of course, from making the paper profitable, which means maximizing circulation, which means conforming to and reinforcing the majority view in the community. A conservative policy is thus imposed willy-nilly, whether it means reinforcing segregationism in the American South or integrationism in the North. Moreover, in the Westminster Press group, for one, it sometimes happens that the same leader column appears in newspapers hundreds of miles apart.

In any case, it is disingenuous to think that editors can simply ignore the character of their proprietors, mediated through the local managers. Just as ordinary journalists are subject to the social controls of those they work with and for, rather than directly seeking the readers' approval,[1] so editors must, consciously or not, hope to produce a paper that will satisfy their bosses not only in profit but also in character. Would a Thomson editor last long if he ran a provincial paper, even a profitable one, that persistently attacked *The Times*, *Sunday Times*, Scottish TV, the growth of newspaper chain-ownership, or the philosophy of advanced capitalism?

*　　*　　*

The growth of chain-ownership would be less dismaying if there were evidence that the proprietors were trying to relieve other forces of homogenization.

For obvious reasons, the provincial press has always had to rely more heavily than the national on agency reporting of foreign news (by Reuter) and of national news (by the Press Association, which is controlled by provincial proprietors). The morning provincials especially have always carried a lot of general news; all in

---

[1] See, for example, 'Social Control in the Newsroom: A Functional Analysis' by Warren Breed, in *Social Forces*, vol. 33, May 1955.

like competition with the London dailies, they are obliged to offer themselves as alternative mirrors of the world at large. By long tradition, morning papers are more serious than evenings, and the best provincial morning papers are no less serious than *The Times*. Their dependence on syndicated reporting is slightly mitigated by the fact that, going to press well after midnight, they occasionally catch important stories that arrived too late for the local editions of the London papers. The effect of emphasizing mostly syndicated news, however, is that the provincial morning papers tend to resemble each other in content until you reach the distinctive, but subordinated, local stuff down the front page or inside. The effect is less obvious in the evening papers, though even in them syndicated reporting is more prominent than it used to be, partly, no doubt, to compete with television news.

Publishers are twitchy on this question. 'Despite its size and its national news coverage it remains very much the local newspaper . . . truly a family newspaper', says one publisher, addressing potential advertisers. Some papers dress up agency news to make it look like their own, by rewrites under the name of its own reporters, or by printing the name of the agency correspondent without accrediting him, so that readers might believe that 'John Robertson reporting from Kuala Lumpur' or 'Garcia Lopez in Lisbon' really are dedicated *Glossop Beast* men cabling the stuff in from the outposts.

Recently there has also been a sharp increase, particularly in the evening papers, in the provincials' use of feature material supplied by specialist agencies in London. Any kind of feature, from cookery, crosswords and cartoons to topical opinion columns, may appear, identically illustrated, in more than a score of unrelated papers up and down the country. The springing-up of feature agencies has been one of the most striking, least noticed developments in journalism during the 1960s. In an 'affluent' period, all newspapers have grown steadily fatter with advertising, and to maintain a decent proportion of editorial columns has meant finding more and more material to fill them with. Agencies offer the provincial features editor a very cheap source of filling matter, some of it by people of a status (e.g. Norman Hartnell, George Best, Milton Shulman) that he could seldom afford to hire on his own. In ruthless competition with one another, offering cut-price package deals, the agencies are also in competition with the syndication departments of the London papers, who are generally the cheapest of all.

K

In local news and comment, the special pressures on a provincial journalist are, up to a point, beneficial. His concept of responsibility has to be much more literal than a national newspaperman's: he is likely to have to respond, face to face, to those he has written about, or to his readers. The same condition, however, is liable to make him think at least twice before writing critically of a councillor or businessman whom he meets regularly in his work, or whom his editor or directors may know at the golf club. The result of criticism could be not just embarrassment but withholding of news. This situation is comparable to that of a correspondent in Washington or, a less severe case, in the London Lobby; with the difference that there the correspondent at least has the chance of supporting action from his colleagues. The provincial specialist will quite often not have colleagues on his beat.

The most celebrated recent example of a provincial newspaper that went ahead and exposed malpractice in its town's arteries was the Sheffield *Morning Telegraph*'s 'rhino-whip' disclosures about the local police in 1963. It would be nice to think that the comparative rarity of such sensations is a tribute to the incorruptibility of local government and business.

Whereas the London papers must, if only for marketing reasons, distinguish themselves from each other, by appearance or politics or both, no such incentive operates in the provinces (always excepting Glasgow and Belfast). In fact there is a good deal of variety in provincial designs, and several of the big ones readily stand comparison with the best dressed London papers. The bold coherence of the *Liverpool Daily Post*, for one, regularly shames the mess of most Fleet Street mosaics. The weight of advertising, however, occupying about 55–60 per cent of the paper on average, homogenizes the look of most provincial papers. Display panels for consumer goods may occasionally be distributed through the provinces; far more constant in every provincial paper, especially the evenings, are the massed pages of small ads, as many as 20 pages sometimes. They are the bread and butter of the provincial evenings' income, and much of the jam too. National papers regard them greedily, and make efforts to build up their own small-ad sections. Churlishly, one is bound to remark that up to half a paper filled with small ads for houses, cars and jobs does nothing to distinguish one town's voice from another's. As in their reliance on syndicated news, there is no obvious way in which the provincial papers might solve small-ad greyness (short of the unthinkable step of limiting them, or even syphoning some off to support a rival paper); but, as Mr Eliot once intoned, we must witness, ere we die, that these things are not otherwise, but thus.

* * *

It is in their politics – their whole attitude to society, not just party preferences – that the provincial papers are most stereotyped. There is, as far as I can see, no longer any such thing as a radical provincial paper, still less a paper of the left.[1]

Indeed, it would be surprising if there were. Once a paper, or grouped pair of papers, is established as the sole press in town, the temptation to avoid minority appeals, to preserve the consensus, is apparently irresistible. It is scarcely possible to please everybody all the time, but the tamer option, of eschewing displeasure to all but the extreme fringes, is normal. A simulacrum of political vigour can be kept up by appeals to the unfissiparous virtues of order, common sense, local pride, respectability, and family-centredness. Ian Jackson found that in the provincial press 'the community's "good" is, in practice, closely identified with the good of the local institutions and local commerce' and that, in consequence, 'it typically demands discipline in relation to penology and education; it values conventions and traditions, and the sanctity of private property. Broadly speaking, it endorses capitalistic assumptions and the protestant ethic.' He quotes the *West Lancashire Evening Gazette*:

> . . . we have an excellent police force in Blackpool, and the magistrates are increasing penalties satisfactorily.
>
> A little sunshine, bringing rather better temper all round, might do as much good as anything.
>
> Plus a touch of the birch, as the chairman of the local bench has been saying.

A conservative consensus prevails in the provincial press, and a good many of them, notably among the morning papers, are, avowedly or not, Conservative with a capital C. A special political pressure is exerted on the morning papers by the economics

---

[1] There was approximately 5 per cent provincial-paper support for Labour in the 1966 general election, according to calculations by Ian Jackson, of the University of Salford, in a study, not yet published, of the provincial press, completed at Birmingham University in 1968. Data and comment supplied by Mr Jackson have been of assistance throughout this chapter.

of advertising, which has driven them into being, broadly, businessmen's papers. To be a popular paper would entail a hopeless fight for national popular advertising with the mass-circulation London morning papers; instead, they rely largely on a prestige audience to attract local business concerns, which would not smile on a local paper pitted against the Tory Party. A degree of independence of big business through page upon page of small ads, like their evening sisters, is ruled out by the assumption that people have little time for small-ad reading until the evening.

Yet the desire to avoid a minority personality persists even in these business-oriented morning papers. Only deviance is openly attacked; the broad mass of voters, Labour or Conservative, are assumed to share a denominator of common sense that is somehow above naked party argument, and entirely tolerant of businessmen's ideals. A peculiarly revealing example appeared some years ago in the Bristol *Western Daily Press*. A Chippenham reader asked:

> In your issue of March 30 you state on page 9 that your Board has laid down as part of your paper's general policy: 'It is independent in its editorial policy and owes allegiance to no political party.'
>
> On page 8 of the same issue . . . the following three paragraphs appear: 'Britain today is in danger of another dose of Socialism with all its implications of bureaucratic waste, incompetence and twisted dogma.
>
> 'One day the Liberals may replace the Socialists. It will be a great day for this country when they do.
>
> 'For the present our hope is in a Tory revival.'
>
> Will you please tell the readers how you square the two items?

The paper did the decent thing. Here is its reply, in full:

> The Western Daily Press is entirely independent and owes no allegiance to any political party. It is however opposed to Socialism precisely for the reasons Mr. Vince quotes from our leader. The Socialists will get as good a hearing as the Tories or Liberals.
>
> And the news will always be kept away from comment and presented with all the dispassionate dynamism and honesty for which the Western Daily Press is now famed.

Two months later the paper declared: 'The Western Daily Press basically supports the Conservative Party.' (What, then, did owing 'no allegiance' mean? – not actually taking money?) On another day, however, the policy was subtly altered again: 'The Western Daily Press is the most independent newspaper in Britain.'

It would be quite wrong to suggest that those posturings are at all typical of the provincial press, or of the provincial mornings in particular; the *WDP* had recently undergone a total change of character, from a 12,000-sale fatalism to an energetic grabbing of an audience now touching 60,000. What is shared by most provincial papers, however, is the underlying motive of occupying the widest political field short of areas of hostility to business ideals. The generality describe themselves as Independent. Independent of what? To be formally independent of any particular political party might be thought a vain sort of independence when the most important political divisions seldom divide the House of Commons. The Independent press is utterly dependent, on advertising; politically, it is utterly committed to a state of affairs in which communication is a commodity, subject to the market, not to the human right to know and say. Its conservative consensus denies readers any encouragement to real argument and participation in decisions which, cumulatively, have a deep influence on what it is like to live in their community. 'A mood is created in which all decisions seem inevitable and in which people speaking of different solutions seem remote and impractical. It is a mood of submission, under the pressures of an effectively occupying power.'[1]

When I put that argument to a provincial proprietor recently, he answered that his papers are always open to the expression of dissentient views; the trouble was finding people to express them. The depressing thing was that he felt apparently no alarm. His father was one of the leaders of a group of Bristol citizens who organized resistance in 1932, when Rothermere and the Berrys had reached a private settlement to avoid costly strife in the provinces. Bristol was Rothermere's portion, the *Evening World* his new paper. The *Evening Post*, Bristol's own reply, was so successful that within a few years it bought Rothermere out, and ran both papers in rivalry until 1962. The *Post* still carries the legend, 'The paper all Bristol asked for and helped to create'. A victor's ideology? Even though circulation is 184,000, dissentient views are hard to find.

[1] Raymond Williams, *The Listener*, 31 July 1969.

*   *   *

For every McLuhanite voice proclaiming the advent of the electronic global village there are, in Britain now, a hundred declaring that regional cultures are alive and . . . well, worth cultivating. The provincial daily paper is a most obvious medium for the expression of distinctive cultures. Yet a striking fact about these papers is precisely how little they smell of particular localities. Consensus is the deodorant. The local smell went when the habit of scepticism went.

'Ideally,' Ian Jackson writes, 'some features of this conservatism need to be challenged at the local level through the restoration of competitive situations – with one of the competing newspapers speaking from a broadly-based radical position. One has in mind the antithesis between the conservative Coleridge and the radical Bentham that John Stuart Mill felt to be so beneficial to society at large – "the one pressing the new doctrines to their utmost consequences; the other reasserting the best meaning and purposes of the old".'

Preaching an ethic of competitive business, the provincial papers engage in scarcely any competition between themselves, except in Glasgow, Belfast, and a few small areas where circulations overlap. Most provincial evening papers capture two-thirds of the local population, and in big cities close on 90 per cent. New papers are inserted only at the points of weakest competition, maximum profitability. It is not a question of supplying the market but of organizing it.

The chain-proprietors defend amalgamation on the grounds that it cuts costs and promotes survival. It habitually assists those ends to the extent of a very comfortable profit indeed. Although it is true that a merger of hands makes industrial sense, newspapers are not hands, but voices.

The situation is one that almost everybody professes to regret. Provincial journalists themselves, especially, often say how much they miss the old spur of trying to beat the local rival on a story (though they can still sometimes compete with the local national-paper men, if they aren't themselves stringers for most of Fleet Street). No journalist can feel too secure when to lose his job would mean moving to another town, instead of hoping to talk his way into the rival organization. Not all provincial journalists, nor all the best, are waiting impatiently to get into Fleet Street.

The family readership is traditionally sceptical of the local rag, with its stagey pix and puff; but in naming streets and people they see every day, providing fodder for gossip or debate, and supplying practical information, it has offered them an enjoyable daily transaction with the community, a confirmation of their belonging to it. Progressive homogenization will breed not scepticism but real boredom: with the anonymous paper, and then with the community's affairs.

There is only one man who has no grounds at all for complaint about wet blanket-coverage: the advertiser, who, controlling two-thirds of the provincial papers' income, is ultimately responsible for the situation, and whom 'one big shopper' would suit to perfection.

12

Correspondent's course

PETER BRUSSE

When I first became a London correspondent (just a month before Mr Wilson became Prime Minister) I found myself faced with a difficult job, and one that was not altogether what I had expected. This was to resist the demands of my editor in Amsterdam for daily news stories and, not just for reasons of laziness, to write as little as possible. I used to ring up my editor every night before bedtime and assure him that there really was no news. I used to tell him that, though one day the British Isles may sink into the sea, *my* feet were still dry. 'I know you won't believe me,' I would say, 'but I swear that there are Britons who are still working. Yes, of course, there are escapes from prison, but Her Majesty has still got *some* of her subjects behind bars. And not *all* the cages of London Zoo are empty: one Goldie doesn't make London into a jungle.'

But my pleading in those years – 1965–7 – was mostly in vain. Every day the English newspapers on my editor's desk proved that I was wrong. Britain *was* going to the dogs, and my editor threatened that if I continued to withhold my labour then he would break my strike by using agency reports. Even the agencies, which were not so alarming as the newspapers, were still enough to make the Dutch fear the worst for Britain.

Dutch friends who came to England during the seamen's strike brought us fresh vegetables because they understood that in England everyone was suffering and on the brink of scurvy. But instead of finding a nation under siege, they saw a country watching a most entertaining game. Papers printed photographs of the strike leader relaxed and playing with his son's toy sailing boat at the edge of a pond. Smiles everywhere, and nobody seemed to think that it was a serious situation.

Britain's image abroad was not made by us foreign correspondents but by the British press. This is an institution for whose tradition I had the highest esteem when I arrived here. The British press was of such high quality and was so well-informed that it was inconceivable to imagine that it might be wrong. So I thought when I was first sent to work in Fleet Street, the Mecca of world journalism. But bathing in the holy river, the Fleet (nowadays used, incidentally, for sewage), I began to have doubts.

An eager colleague of mine had said to me, 'It's marvellous working here in Fleet Street. We have 25,000 journalists at our disposal, and so we have as many good stories as we want. It's just a question of translating. There's nowhere else in the world where you would find this.'

But, stubbornly, I began to argue that the British press had failed to adjust to the new realities of life. In spite of all their fierce attacks on Mr Wilson, on the Trade Unions and other scapegoats, they still think, I told my colleague, that nothing can really be wrong in their country. They are a superior race, and attacking one another is their national sport, just as the Spanish have bullfighting. Look how furious they get, I said, when a mere foreigner dares to criticize Britain. We are not allowed to understand them, and anyway we can't be taken seriously because we have no sense of humour.

Patiently I waited for the day when the British press (and Britain) would realize that playtime was over. I went on not sending stories to my paper, feeling like the little Dutch boy with his finger in the dyke. But it was useless. The Dutch were reading more and more British papers and Holland was flooded with bad news from England (as there are no Sunday papers in Holland, the British Sundays, especially *The Observer*, are widely read).

In the end I learnt the expression, 'If you can't beat 'em, join 'em' and decided to follow that advice. I removed my finger from the dyke and applied it to my typewriter. I wrote more and more, and to my pride was even quoted by *The Times* for sneering at the 'Victorian London docks'. My editor became so enthusiastic that he wanted to come and see for himself the orgy of Swinging London set in the agony of Britannia's deathbed.

Then, quite unexpectedly, things changed; help came, and from

L

an unexpected quarter, namely Printing House Square. When *The Times* put news on its front page, suddenly all its infallibility disappeared. Its very first front-page story – 'London to be new HQ for Nato' – was nonsense and everyone abroad knew it. *The Times*, perhaps unknowingly, had done a great service to Britain, and from that moment the press abroad dared to agree with Mr Macmillan who had said that the nice thing about *The History of The Times* was that it showed how mistaken *The Times* had been in the past. And loss of faith in the credibility of *The Times* spread to the rest of the British press.

Nowadays Britain is going out of the picture. My editor is no longer interested in whether I get wet feet or not. I find it more and more difficult to get my stories on politics, the economy, the balance of payments, etc., printed. My readers seem to be as bored with these subjects as they are with Swinging London (certainly since we had a girl on Dutch television announcing a pop-programme completely in the nude and no Mevrouw Marie Withuis wrote in to complain). In the good old days readers used to write letters telling me that Montgomery was a year older than I had said he was, or asking me to explain what a shadow cabinet is ('something to do with British ghosts?'). But recently a story headlined 'Come-back for Mother Brown' (it should of course have been Brother, i.e. George, Brown) failed to produce any reaction. Nowadays, if I am desperately in need of some response, the only thing I can do is to write a story about abortions. These, far from abortive, give birth to bags of mail. But, alas, Holland is going to have its own abortion clinics, so I shall have to find something else to write about.

Now that Britain is becoming a country comparable with others, we foreigners no longer see it as a mortal sin to say what we think about Britain. The only trouble now is that the British seem to listen to foreigners – and I hate to be listened to. But, to skip the generalities about Britain as a whole, I will concentrate on the press, which is as irritating, lovable, contradictory, a-logical, puzzling and intriguing as all English institutions. And, like everything in this country, an institution is what it is. For that reason alone the British press is different from that of any other country.

Of course in other countries people also read newspapers, just as in other countries people go out for a drink, drive cars, keep pets and do a bit of gardening. But it is only in Britain that everything from the daily pinta milk to the hot water bottle is treated as a ceremony wrapped up in traditional rules. In what other country could casualness (how do you translate this word into another language?) mean formality, and casual dress mean uniform for the weekend.

The British people have a genius for putting magic into the most irrelevant thing, and therefore every foreign correspondent coming to this country is confronted with the fundamental question of whether Fleet Street is the Emperor without any clothes? It is curious to notice the extent to which all London correspondents of foreign newspapers become involved in the British press we seem to hate and love so intensely.

I thought it would be interesting to ask my fellow London correspondents what they felt about the British press. The first thing that struck me was how much easier it is to get an interview with the editor of *The Times* or *Daily Mirror* than with most of my colleagues. Was it self-defence? Or was it self-importance in a country where foreign correspondents don't count, where they have to cover Parliament well separated from the real (i.e., British) press in the Press Gallery?

Anyway, one foreign correspondent said he couldn't see me this week 'because of the TUC Conference'. No, he wasn't going down to Brighton; he was going to cover the Conference from his office in Fleet Street. A French colleague was only to be found in his very English club. The wife of a German correspondent thought I wanted to speak to her son because I had not asked to speak to '*Dr* So-and-So'. The chief correspondent of *Frankfurter Allgemeine Zeitung* had his doubts about whether or not to see me and, after consultation with his superiors in Frankfurt, decided not to: 'If the readers can have it straight from the horse's mouth, why should I give it to you?' he said enigmatically. He was also afraid I might misquote him. I praised him for his deep knowledge of his profession.

The *Bild-Zeitung* people were rather reserved when I asked to speak to their boss, but when I explained that I would like to discuss the British press, they were jubilant: 'Of course, he is *just* the man to speak to.' The *Pravda* correspondent was friendly but said that he thought that as a guest of this country it would be improper for him to discuss the British press. His colleague on *Izvestia*, however, was very helpful. He was prepared to come and see me, but I told him it would be less trouble for him if I came to his flat. When I got there, I was, for the first time in England, treated to real Dutch whisky.

Almost embarrassing in his politeness was Mr Mitsugu Naka-mura of Tokio's *Asahi Shimbun*. When I arrived at his office he had all ready for me a photocopied statement about himself and his influential newspaper taken from a very impressive book on American-Japanese relations.

The most protected correspondent of all turned out to be – to my surprise – Anthony Lewis of the *New York Times*, but once I was admitted to his extremely busy office he was as open, efficient and outspoken as one expects from an American journalist.

To start with the virtues of the British press, they were (my colleagues told me) its professionalism, its wide scope of interests and the variety of papers. 'Four quality papers, c'est unique,' said M. Henri Pierre of the unique *Le Monde* (a paper he described as a 'weekly published daily'). Pierre, after stints in Washington and Moscow and back in London for the second time, sees in the British press 'the best and worst journalism'. He is not too fond of the popular papers, 'worse than in France', but agrees with most others that the *Daily Mirror* is improving. With several others, he prefers the *Financial Times* to *The Times*, which he says is 'no longer up to standard, has lost reliability but is easier to read. This, I think, is an improvement'.

Mitsugu Nakamura does not like the idea of a popular press, and this opinion is shared by others who think the popular press is a result of Britain's poor education system. Mr Nakamura would prefer fewer papers, which might help to bring down the class barriers. 'Now every class and every group has its own paper,' he says. And Daniel Viklund of Stockholm's *Dagens Nyheter* says 'We don't have a popular press. We have everything, serious and popular all together; *Private Eye* and *Country Life* in the same paper.' *Svenska Dagbladet*'s Per Persson agrees that the British press is entrenched in the class system.

Renato Proni, a London correspondent of *La Stampa* of Milan, admires the 'quick style' of British papers, and correspondents of most of the non-anglophone nations agree that the English language is particularly well-suited for journalism. Several col-leagues mentioned the highly developed art of making headlines. Anthony Lewis for one enjoys them, and *Bild-Zeitung*'s Karl-Heinz Kukowski comments that they often have more humour than in Germany: 'We can't do that. Perhaps we are too serious.' For Viklund, the English press is the best written in the world. Pierre, however, has some reservations and has noticed a decline of good writers. The best, perhaps the last, of the good writers seem to congregate in the *Guardian*: 'Alistair Cooke is excellent, but I don't know whether he is appreciated by English readers. And, of course, there is Norman Shrapnel.'

It was interesting to notice that most praise went to the appearance, the lay-out – the shell of the oyster, as someone remarked. To which another added: 'An English newspaper is in the first place a product to be sold; as smooth and slick as is to be expected in the supermarket era.' The calm Daniel Viklund remarked, puffing quietly at his pipe, 'Journalism in Britain is a trade, not a profession.'

Looking at the content of the British press (the pearl itself), criticisms arose, some mild, some less so. 'I detest its vagueness,' said Kukowski, whose *Bild-Zeitung* with four and a half million copies a day never leaves any doubt as to what it thinks of long-haired students, Willy Brandt and other dangers that undermine the state. 'In England,' he says, 'you can write stories without having any facts. Rumours are enough. I hate expressions like "it is understood", "it may", "it is said", etc. Perhaps this has to do with German *tuchtigkeit* (thoroughness). The British press often offers my paper so-called exclusive stories, which are prominently printed in papers like the *Express*, but we can't use them. It's not enough to trace the exiled king of Libya. We want news. In 50 per cent of all cases the British papers don't give enough facts. If, for example, I read that the wife is the owner of the house, I want to know why she is the owner and not her husband' – a remark which seemed to reveal more about patriarchal Germany than about the British press.

Kukowski admires the respect of British journalists for a person's private life. Where his paper is concerned, he said, private life becomes public property much more quickly. His paper, for example, is much more interested in whether a film star is divorced, but homosexuality is taboo.

It was not only Kukowski who spotted vagueness. Persson said: 'The English are good at writing an essay without saying much' and Anthony Lewis thinks 'the English often take too much for granted. When they talk about the largest Union, I am interested to know how many members that Union has.' On the other hand, Proni says: 'We Latins are more philosophical. We use fewer facts than the pragmatic English. We discuss things more philosophically. Perhaps a bit too much so, but the English press lacks thinkers. They talk with many facts about the crisis of the balance of payments. It is not the crisis of balance of payments. It is the crisis of a nation. Look, for example, how they cover the Common Market; all the facts are there, but no more than that. There is no ideology. They don't seem to understand what it is all about.'

Others saw a connection between vagueness and the libel laws, which most thought were ridiculous. 'We, in America, may print almost everything; perhaps we go too far, but here the libel laws certainly are a drawback. It is overdone,' said Anthony Lewis. Pierre Bertrand of *Le Figaro* thought that the libel laws here could be abused to prevent publication, but that in spite of the strict laws the most tasteless divorce stories could still be printed freely. This, he said, is disgusting. In Holland and permissive Sweden one never finds reports of divorce cases and Viklund said it was quite a problem for the Swedish papers as to whether they could inform their readers that Ingrid Bergman had got divorced. Some people in Sweden, in fact, announce their divorce in an advertisement.

Most correspondents think that it is much easier to gather news in their own countries. Therefore papers in England are bound to be vague. For one thing there is the lobby-system, which is loathed by foreign correspondents, and not in the first place because we foreigners can't be members of the club. The lobby-system is, I think, a highly sophisticated form of censorship. Bertrand wouldn't go so far as to say that the British press was censored, but it was 'orientated'. Kobysh of *Izvestia*, however, did think there was censorship. The British press was a capitalist press and defended the capitalist system under cover of being 'objective'. He had challenged a press lord to publish a socialist view on the German problem, but this had not been done. The Soviet press defended communism, but it didn't claim to be objective. You knew where it stood. There was no such thing as objectivity, he said.

Because of the lack of information (especially political information) journalists here have to find their own news, and therefore the British press contains large amounts of speculation. Papers very often seem to be more interested in what *may* happen than in what *has* happened. We hear about 'inevitable' clashes in the Cabinet, the Trade Unions, etc., but very often nothing happens and everyone forgets all about it. Not exceptionally, papers fail to report the very non-event they have been building up for weeks. One of the most notorious examples, of course, was the series of warming-up stories for the 27 October demonstration in 1968 which *The Times* printed on its front pages. And I remember a big story in the *Guardian* announcing a strike of a handful of international telephone operators. There were, the *Guardian* admitted, not many people involved: but those few, the reader was told in real Battle of Britain language, could paralyse British exports because they would cut off all overseas telephone communications. The damage eventually done appeared to be negligible.

One could argue, of course, that such stories are meant as deterrents and warnings, but I doubt it. I think it is better explained by the British taste for sensation: 'In England there are no reporters left, only dramatists,' Viklund said.

During the tragi-comedy of devaluation, it was interesting to see how the press functioned as a sort of lightning conductor on to which the reader could release his rage before going off to work, quietly and composed, all passion spent. In the old days, public hangings kept the masses quiet; now it seems the papers have taken over that cathartic function. I am sure the British morning papers deserve much credit for the easy-going, phlegmatic attitude their readers display during the rest of the day. I must admit that I myself enjoy my breakfast ride through Wonderland, but is this what a national press is for?

Much has happened in the last two years and fortunately a wave of realism has gone through Britain. The press, with the notorious exception of the *Daily Express*, is coming down to earth, where even Britain belongs. The Ulster crisis seems to be an example of this realism. The unsolvable tragedy on Britain's doorstep awoke an involvement unprecedented since, perhaps, Suez. Suddenly it was worth while to send those big teams of reporters (manpower in the British press is unchallenged) to Ulster, and for the first time I did not get the impression that sending all those people was merely a status symbol. How much money and manpower has been wasted on boring party conferences, and what have all those news teams brought back except loads of trivial gossip and speculation?

But real involvement is still rare in British journalism. Perhaps this is due to the cynical attitude of the nation itself. Take Biafra, for example. After more than a year of the war, the British press started to give its attention to Biafra. We got excellent, moving and analytical stories. *The Times* even honoured Biafra by sending Winston Churchill himself, and a leader, in real 'Thunderer' style, followed Churchill's reports. A few days later Parliament debated whether Britain should stop delivering arms to Nigeria.

The debate was a walk-over for the government. The press then seemed to lose interest, and Biafra stories disappeared again.

Why? Is letting off steam once in a while sufficient to clear one's conscience, or is it that readers don't want to be bored with the same story every day? We don't see much campaigning in the British press, partly because in Britain campaigns don't seem to achieve much. It would be impossible in Britain for a paper to have Parliament recalled from summer recess as, Kukowski told me, *Bild-Zeitung* did a few years ago when the German government announced the increase in telephone charges. 'In Italy,' Renato Proni told me, 'newspapers are pressure groups, but here it's all big business. Papers are the vehicles for advertisers.'

Competition amongst the newspapers is fiercer than in most other countries, which is in many ways a good thing. But in some ways the need to attract readers is a serious disadvantage. Papers are obliged to print stories people want to read, and who wants to read unpleasant stories? By unpleasant stories I do not just mean rape, murder and other crimes of violence, because people seem to love reading about them everywhere. No, the unpleasant stories they don't want to print are about the scandals which exist in every country and for which everyone is more or less responsible; the scandals in which all members of an affluent society are to blame; poverty, homelessness, the shameful state of mental hospitals and so on. To these shocking situations the press gives far too little attention.

In general, the papers seem to do their utmost not to disturb their readers, and if reports on these matters are to be printed, scapegoats are immediately found. Findings on accomodation or the treatment of the mentally disturbed are seen as an attack on the Minister responsible and not, as they should be, as a shame to the nation. If Shelter points to the homeless, the papers seem to be more interested in Des Wilson than in the homeless themselves.

Proni says that 'For the British press nothing can be wrong with Britain, and if something goes wrong there is always the stereotype scapegoat. The Unions for example; I hate the phobia against the British striker. The British journalists are lazy, not the workers. Journalists are too lazy to find out what is really wrong in the factories.'

The correspondents of several foreign papers think the British reader does not expect to find the truth in his paper and therefore the press's influence on government and public is less than in many other countries. 'In America, the press is more influential,'

Anthony Lewis says, and mentions the case of Vietnam. He thinks that in political affairs the British press has little or no influence. Its influence is to be found in small things like the choice of a new airport, and Viklund sees the main influence of the press in such matters as where to spend your holiday and how to dress.

And is the British press reliable? Some say yes, others 'where it really matters' or 'to some extent', but Lewis gives an outright 'No'. We spoke the day after a quality Sunday newspaper[1] had carried two front page stories which were, Lewis said, 'outrageous and dangerously untrue'. This sort of irresponsible sensationalism was the product of the competitive pressures on British papers. 'They want to have scoops even when there are no scoops to be found.' He could understand this attitude, but it was nevertheless regrettable and harmful.

'British journalists tend to put their own point of view in their news stories more than is proper,' Lewis commented, but the Latin correspondents don't favour separating news and comment. 'A personal view,' Pierre says, 'stimulates the mind.'

Viklund said: 'Every time I go to an EEC conference in Brussels, when I see the English papers the next day I think they must have been to a different conference.' He gave this example in connection with the insularity of the British press, a topic dear to every foreign correspondent's heart. 'I detest their fantastic insularity,' Proni says, and Nakamura comments that the British papers miss so many important developments in other countries that he has to read foreign papers like *Le Monde*, the *Neue Zürcher Zeitung* and the *New York Times*. He complains about the way Vietnam is covered: 'Too much human interest and much too little analysis.' South America, some correspondents remarked, is non-existent on the map used in Fleet Street, and Asian affairs are not understood. 'Africa,' a Frenchman said, 'does not consist just of former British colonies, as the British assume.' And as far as the Arab countries are concerned, they certainly get less attention than in the German or French press. Anthony Sampson has pointed out in *The New Europeans* how much prominence is given in Britain to domestic news, and Kukowski said: 'It's no longer "Deutschland über Alles" but "Britain über alles"' and he gave – as several others did – examples of the parochial headlines. Sports writers are almost shameless in their chauvinism. And in

[1] On legal advice, I am told that it would be libellous to mention the paper by name: such restrictions by the libel laws, though taken for granted in Britain, are still astonishing to a foreigner.

no other country, I think, does one find headlines like: 'Two British girls injured in Turkish air-crash – 98 people killed.'

Chauvinism is very much part of British coverage of foreign affairs. Viklund calls it 'a very advanced ignorance' and he points out that every meeting between a German and a French minister must – in the eyes of the British press – be pro or anti Britain; an arrogance which, Proni thinks, is a left-over of British imperialism.

Now that Britain's future seems to be found in Europe a lot has improved, but I still cannot see why the 'Crusading *Mirror*', so proud of its Europeanism, does not give more attention to the way of life in the EEC countries. Instead of trying to understand Britain's new friends, the press sticks to old clichés about foreigners and glorifies the Britishness of Britain. I am amazed to see how little interest there is in the way the French and Germans try to solve problems which are no different from the problems in England. And why, for example, are foreign books hardly ever reviewed in the British press? (Even in translation they get nothing like the attention paid to home-grown products.)

But perhaps the British papers are right to help preserve the British outlook and to make national heroes out of people who sail around the world now that Britain can't compete in space. It shows the British genius, and it keeps Britain apart from all those boring, serious countries where the press reflects the idealism, morality and struggle for life of its nation. The British press still has the time to find entertainment in the most serious matters and to draw attention to oddities and eccentricities which in other countries seem to have disappeared altogether. It has become an eccentricity on its own. There is no press in the world you can hate with so much love.

Notes on contributors

Richard Boston was born in 1938. After two years as an art student, he went to King's College, Cambridge, where he read English. He has done English language-teaching in Sicily, Sweden and Paris, and hopes never to have to do so again. A very brief acting career resulted in fleeting appearances in Jacques Tati's *Playtime*. He worked on *Peace News* in Committee of 100 days, and was on the staff of the *Times Literary Supplement* for two years. He now works on *New Society*, of which he is books editor.

Raymond Williams was born in 1921 at the Welsh border village of Pandy, where his father was a railway signalman. He was educated at the village school, at Abergavenny Grammar School, and at Trinity College, Cambridge. After the war, in which he served as an anti-tank captain in the Guards Armoured Division, he became an adult education tutor in the Oxford University Delegacy for Extra-Mural Studies. In 1961 he was elected Fellow of Jesus College, Cambridge, where he is now Reader in Drama. His books include *Drama from Ibsen to Brecht*, *Drama in Performance*, *Culture and Society*, *The Long Revolution*, *Communications*, *Modern Tragedy* and two novels, *Border Country* and *Second Generation*. He is married and has three children.

D. A. N. Jones was born in Wandsworth, 1931, educated at Bec School, Tooting, and Balliol College, Oxford. He worked on the *Oxford Mail and Times* from 1956 to 1958 as general reporter, theatre reviewer and agricultural correspondent. From 1963 to 1965 he was general reporter, feature-writer and industrial correspondent for *Tribune*. From 1965 to 1967 he was assistant literary editor on the *New Statesman*. His reports and reviews have been published by most of the metropolitan newspaper companies, and by several overseas journals. Currently his reviews appear mostly in the *Listener*, the *Times Literary Supplement* and the *New York Review of Books*, while his reports and feature articles appear in the *Radio Times*, the colour supplements and glossy magazines. He is married with four children, and has published two novels, *Parade in Pairs* and *Never Had It So Good*. He prefers *Tribune*, as a working environment, to any other London journal, and wishes he could make a living and get a hearing by writing for *Tribune* alone.

Tom Baistow was born in Glasgow in 1914 and was educated in state schools in Scotland and Canada. He has worked on five national newspapers, mainly the *News Chronicle* (foreign editor) and *Daily Herald* (features editor). As a feature writer he specialized in social matters, but covered everything from the Olympic Games to the Congo war. He has done most jobs on newspapers from reporting to sub-editing to art editing to layout. He is now deputy editor of the *New Statesman* and writes its press column 'Communicators', formerly under the name Magnus Turnstile.

Malcolm Southan is an Oxford graduate who started his newspaper career as an office boy. He has worked as a copy boy on the mass circulation Hearst paper, the *New York Mirror* (which is now dead), and in this country he has worked on provincial papers in Aberdeen, Wolverhampton and Cardiff, and in London on the *Sunday Times* and *The Sun*. He is now a member of Granada Television's *World in Action* team.

Susanne Puddefoot was appointed Women's Page Editor of *The Times* in 1965 and in 1968 won an IPC National Press Award for her work on the women's pages. Educated at Blackpool Collegiate School for Girls and Girton College, Cambridge, her previous career has included working as an advertising copywriter, London correspondent of the American arts magazine *Horizon* and film critic of *The Times Educational Supplement*. She is currently working on a book on the women's press.

Geoffrey Nicholson was born in 1929, and was educated at Swansea Grammar School and University College, Swansea, where he read English. After coming to London, he spent four years as a copywriter in Crawfords Advertising. Since then, apart from short spells as sports features editor at the *Sunday Times* and as would-be editor of an IPC sports magazine that never came out, he has worked as a freelance journalist. He contributes regularly on sport to *The Observer* and the *Guardian*, and on other subjects to *Management Today*, the *Sunday Times Magazine*, *Nova*, *Radio Times*, etc. He has written *Report on Rugby* (Heinemann, 1959) with John Morgan, and *The Professionals* (André Deutsch, 1964). He lives in north London; married; three sons.

John Palmer is 31. He has been in journalism for twelve years, seven of them as an economics and financial journalist. At present he writes on economic affairs for the *Guardian*. He has long been active in left-wing politics and is a member of the International Socialists and the editorial board of their weekly paper, *Socialist Worker*.

Peter Fryer was born at Cottingham, near Hull, in 1927. A shop steward in a pottery factory at 18, he was dismissed by the *Yorkshire Post* in 1947 because of his membership of the Communist Party. From 1948 he worked for the *Daily Worker* as parliamentary and occasional foreign correspondent, resigning in 1956 when the paper suppressed his dispatches from Budapest during the Hungarian revolution. His books include *Mrs Grundy: Studies in English Prudery* (Dobson, 1963), *The Birth Controllers* (Secker and Warburg, 1965), and *Private Case – Public Scandal* (Secker and Warburg, 1966). He is an occasional contributor to *Encounter* and *New Society*.

A. C. H. Smith is a freelance writer, living in Bristol. He was born in London in 1935, went to Cambridge and then into journalism. In Bristol he founded and edited an arts page in the *Western Daily Press*; when the page was suppressed 'for economic reasons' he quit, and freelanced as Royal Shakespeare Company programme compiler and a *Times* cricket correspondent. From 1965–8 he was at the Centre for Contemporary Cultural Studies, Birmingham University, as senior research associate on the Rowntree project on the popular press. He has written for television, films, has published poetry and a novel, *The Crowd* (1965).

Peter Brusse was born in Rotterdam in 1936. He took his degree
in law at Amsterdam University and decided to become the first
intellectual in his family of artists, actors and film-makers. Having
failed to do so, he became a journalist. He spent a few years on
De Haagse Post, a weekly once described as a mixture of *Time*
Magazine and *Private Eye*. In 1964 he joined *De Volkskrant*
('People's Daily'), a national paper which *Guardian*-readers
exiled to Holland would be happy to read. *De Volkskrant* sent
him to London in September 1964 and promised him it would be
for no more than one year. He is still here. He also broadcasts for
Dutch radio and has published in Holland a guide to London which
is read by as many Dutch diplomats as hippies: 'Something must
be wrong with it,' he says.